THE PASTOR AS MORAL GUIDE

CREATIVE PASTORAL CARE AND COUNSELING

THE PASTOR
AS MORAL GUIDE

Rebekah L. Miles

FORTRESS PRESS MINNEAPOLIS

THE PASTOR AS MORAL GUIDE

Cover design: Brad Norr
Cover: "Sailboat," anonymous painting created between 1942 and 1944 by a child in the Terezin concentration camp; original now housed in the archives of the State Jewish Museum in Prague; published in . . . I Never Saw Another Butterfly . . . (New York: Schocken Books, 1993), pp. 56–57; used courtesy of the United States Holocaust Memorial Museum.

Library of Congress Cataloging-in-Publication Data

Miles, Rebekah, 1960–
    The pastor as moral guide / Rebekah Miles.
        p.   cm. — (Creative pastoral care and counseling)
    Includes bibliographical references.
    ISBN 0-8006-3136-6 (alk. paper)
    1. Pastoral theology. 2. Christian ethics. 3. Pastoral counseling. I. Title.
II. Series: Creative pastoral care and counseling series.
BV4011.5.M485   1999
253 — dc21   98-48893
                                                                              CIP

Manufactured in the U.S.A.   AF 1-3136

03   02   01   00   99   1   2   3   4   5   6   7   8   9   10

To Len

CONTENTS

EDITOR'S FOREWORD

Every Christian individual is an ethicist, every Christian pastor a moral guide. Moral guidance, a crucial part of all ministry, is particularly important in pastoral care. These are key assertions of *The Pastor as Moral Guide*.

The author, Rebekah Miles, is a critic of pastoral care that is either too flabby or too stern. She calls to task pastoral care that (like much psychotherapy) takes an ethically neutral stance; likewise she challenges pastoral care that is morally harsh and fails to offer compassion along with guidance. She is especially concerned about pastoral care that relies on self-fulfillment as its guiding ethical metaphor—recognizing that all guidance we do as pastors will be "tainted by sin" but urging us still to offer guidance, always being attentive to God, who guides us in our guiding.

In *The Pastor as Moral Guide*, Miles presents a style of moral guidance "in the muddled middle." It is a way to address ethical issues without becoming moralistic. She seriously discusses moral issues in pastoral ministry and especially in pastoral-care situations typical to the parish, offering suggested methods for talking with parishioners caught in a moral dilemma.

This book is a breath of moral fresh air in a smoggy psychological atmosphere. The style is clear and concrete. I have read it several times, each time in a single sitting, and have enjoyed its clear prose and its thoughtful approach to giving moral guidance.

The introduction of *The Pastor as Moral Guide* addresses the reluctance that many of us feel toward offering moral guidance. Chapter 1 presents maps of the moral landscape and discusses the various families of ethics, especially rule and goal ethics, and how they relate to pastoral caregiving. It also suggests four questions that pastors can use as they guide parishioners. Chapter 2 looks at the steps for moral guidance in pastoral care and provides a number of specific methods, or exercises. Chapters 3, 4, and 5 address three common areas of pastoral care that frequently call for moral guidance: chapter 3, work; chapter 4, marriage and divorce; and chapter 5, sexual misconduct and how ministers and churches can develop accountability in that area.

I am certain that you will find in *The Pastor as Moral Guide* much to strengthen and enrich your pastoral care, counseling, and general ministry. It will help you to guide your parishioners in ways that are not only therapeutic, but moral.

—HOWARD W. STONE

ACKNOWLEDGMENTS

But human excellence grows like a vine tree, fed by the green dew, raised up, among wise men [sic] *and just, to the liquid sky.*
—Pindar (Nussbaum 1986, 1)

This book is about tending goodness and nourishing moral excellence. It assumes that we flourish and grow as moral people, as Christians, with the help and guidance of others—of pastors, friends, family, neighbors, and Sunday School teachers. Comparing the growth of human character to a plant, philosopher Martha Nussbaum reflects on the line by the Greek poet Pindar quoted above:

> The excellence of the good person . . . is like a young plant: something growing in the world, slender, fragile, in constant need of food from without . . . it needs fostering weather . . . as well as the care of concerned and intelligent keepers, for its continued health and full perfection. So, the poet suggests, do we (Nussbaum 1986, 1).

We come to be good people with the help and care of others. For most of us, this claim is no abstract theory; it is the most basic fact of our lives. Like Pindar's plant, we've been nourished, and shaded. If there is one bit of goodness in us, that's because it was carefully tended by good souls around us. That's true for my life. It's also true for this book.

Like neighborhood garden plots, most books are community efforts. They and their makers are tended, shaded, pruned, and nourished. My book and I are no exception; we have had loads of help and care. I am grateful for the tending and support given by my colleagues at Brite Divinity School, Texas Christian University, particularly my dean, Leo Perdue, and associate deans Mark Toulouse and Toni Craven. The faculty at Brite responded to the introduction at a faculty colloquium. Students in introductory classes and my "Moral Guides" seminar read early drafts. I thank them and other readers including Don and Carol Browning, E. Clinton Gardner, Bonnie Miller-McLemore, Darryl Trimiew, Howard Stone, Mary Hill, Len Delony, Jo Ann and John Miles, John Miles, Jean Burnham, Shirley Bubar, and especially administrative assistant Sherry Willis and my graduate assistants, Pam Rose-Beeler and Melanie Moore.

Friends talked me through the writing and revising of this and other projects—especially Lois Malcolm, Susan Simonaitis, Susan White, and Charlene Galarneau. I was cheered by the good-natured sympathy of parents, siblings, cousins, nieces, nephews, aunts, and uncles. They knew (usually) when to practice radical intervention or benign neglect. I am grateful to the Little Rock Annual Conference of the United Methodist Church and my bishop, Janice Riggle Huie, who appoints me to write and teach (and who also read the manuscript). Thanks go to Michael West, Henry French, Deborah Brandt, and others at Fortress Press for their help with editing. I owe thanks and more to the editor of this series, Howard Stone, whose care for this book most often took the form of pruning and cutting. (The manuscript was originally twice its present length.) As his friend and colleague, I have been the recipient of good advice, great company, fine meals, and (as one link in a continuing chain of practical jokes) an old goat named John Wesley (which Stone himself delivered to my ethics class in the middle of a lecture on Martin Luther's understanding of the law. The lecture was never completed because the Wesley goat ate my lecture notes).

This book is dedicated to my husband, Len Delony, who is a hospital chaplain and has graduate degrees in pastoral care and counseling as well as social work. On the pastoral care side, then, this book is more about his field than mine. And even on the Christian ethics side, while I may lay claim to it as an academic specialty, Len embodies Christian ethics in his life. I talk about ethics; Len simply goes about doing good. I'm happy to be a principal beneficiary of his goodness. Len not only tended this book, he also tends and nourishes me; more important, he reminds me to rest in the shade of God's abundant grace.

But for all the tending and care, pruning and shaping by these delightful people, they are not responsible if the yield is poor. If the vine is a bit weak, the fruit too green, or the leaves a little shriveled, don't blame them. The fault lies not with the neglect of my fellow gardeners, but with the intractable nature of the materials with which they were working—that is to say, me.

And in the end, of course, even if the fruit is off or the yield low in any of the efforts of our ministries—whether writing books or guiding parishioners—our weakness is never the final word. Twenty-six hundred years ago—give or take a few decades—a disappointed prophet (or his frustrated editor) left us a testimony for dealing with poor harvests. Though it goes against my competitive nature and perfectionist training, I keep trying to remind myself that he's right.

> Though the fig tree does not blossom, and no fruit is on the vines; though the produce of the olive fails and the fields yield no food; though the flock is cut off from the fold and there is no herd in the stalls, yet I will rejoice in the Lord; I will exult in the God of my salvation. (Hab. 3:17-18)

Nussbaum may be correct. Perhaps our moral goodness depends on the attention and care of others and on the luck of circumstance. But in the end, what matters most is not our goodness or excellence, but God's. What matters most is not our power to tend and guide, but God's power to save and love. Whatever our success or failure as moral guides and moral people, all is enfolded in the tender love of God. This book is about both sides—about the importance of human responsibility and about the abundance of God's grace—no matter what. This book talks about the ways that we Christians must shape, nourish, and guide each other. It calls us to guide other fellow pilgrims. Guidance matters. It makes a difference in the people we become and the lives we lead. But our success as moral guides and moral people is never the final word. The final word is God's abundant love. When we remember that, we will be able to join Habakkuk's song of praise. We will rejoice in the Lord. We will exult in the God of our salvation.

INTRODUCTION

May the God of peace . . . hold me by my right hand, and guide me . . . Who is a Shepherd to shepherds and a Guide to guides: that we may feed [God's] flock with knowledge.

—Nazianzen 1995, 227

Every Christian is an ethicist—asking questions, making choices, and learning to live responsibly. And every pastor is both an ethicist and an ethical teacher, a moral guide. These claims are true for ancient times and our time. In our time, we face a crisis of moral responsibility: Many find it hard to discern responsibilities and easy to shirk them. This crisis of responsibility demands moral guidance. Many parishioners look to pastors for help when they face questions of moral responsibility. Because of the needs of the community and the calling of God, pastors cannot responsibly avoid moral guidance. In sermons, Sunday school lessons, youth trips, and many other tasks, pastors guide. Pastoral counseling is no exception. How will pastors fulfill their responsibilities as moral guides?

When I ask pastors about their ordinary working days, I hear story after story of people facing moral crisis. In pastoral counseling sessions, coffee shops, and hospital waiting rooms, pastors and parishioners meet ethical issues head-on. A large family gathers in the surgery waiting room of the county hospital, trying to decide if they should put grandmother on life support machines. A middle-aged husband who is having an affair tells the pastor that he does not know how to stop and is not sure he wants to stop. A member of the junior high church youth group is three months pregnant; she sits in the pastor's office crying, struggling to choose from a handful of tough options. An inner-city mother worries that her children will be shot by gangs or by the police and asks what she and her church could do to make their neighborhood a safer place. A young corporate lawyer wonders how she has ended up working eighty-hour weeks for a company she does not believe in. A couple sits in the pastor's office talking about divorce, while their daughters swing on the church playground visible beyond the office window.

For pastors, these are not simply hypothetical cases, but real stories of people in their care. The questions raised are not just abstract matters from an academic textbook, but immediate matters of the heart. Whether the issue is adultery, divorce, racism, living wills, teen pregnancy, or white-collar crime, pastors stand by people who are struggling and confused, and pastors struggle with them.

1

As a pastor of rural and urban churches, and now as a seminary professor to student pastors, I have heard more ethics cases than I care to remember. If I have heard hundreds of cases in the last few years, no doubt pastors with many years in ministry have seen thousands of people struggle and have heard thousands of stories. What haunts me haunts many pastors: We remember not just the technical, ethical features of the cases, but the pain in the voices of the people we are called to serve. We remember the confused faces. We're haunted by persistent self-questioning. "What might I have done differently?" "Could I have said anything to convince that father to stay with his wife and children?" "If I had acted more quickly, might that child have been spared further abuse?" These are painful questions, because they are about the tragedies of particular people in our care and come with the memories of distinct faces, voices, and moments.

Moral guidance is a crucial part of the ministry of pastoral care. Some pastoral caregivers and scholars have attempted to avoid moral judgments and remain neutral. Others have steered themselves away from the values and virtues of Christian traditions and have opted for a more secular focus on personal self-fulfillment and happiness. This book assumes that pastoral care cannot avoid moral judgment, that moral neutrality is impossible, and that the value of self-fulfillment alone does not make a Christian ethic. The pastoral caregiver is a Christian moral guide; that skin cannot be shed. The question is, How will the pastor guide? Confronted by the widespread failure of responsibility, how will pastors fulfill their responsibilities?

MORAL GUIDANCE IN THE MUDDLED MIDDLE

"How do you guide a church member who is having an affair?" With this simple question I ignited a furious argument among pastors at a workshop I was leading on ethics and pastoral care. I was caught off guard by the reaction. In the earlier sessions, the more liberal pastors had championed the prophetic role of the pastor to speak against classism, sexism, and oppression. They were ready to challenge these evils anytime, anywhere. Their conservative colleagues were more cautious. "There are different views on these issues," they said. "Judge not, that ye not be judged."

But when I asked about offering guidance to a parishioner committing adultery, strange things happened. Many of the pastors began to backpedal; their positions reversed. The more conservative pastors, who had been so cautious about judging classism and sexism, reminded us of the Biblical prohibitions against marital infidelity. They called for pastors to speak prophetically, opposing adultery in their preaching, teaching, and counseling. They were ready to challenge sexual infidelity anytime, anywhere. The liberal pastors were incensed. "We shouldn't focus on legalistic rules, but should find out what the parishioner needs," they said. "We shouldn't impose the Christian story, but should listen sympathetically to the parishioner's story." "Judge not that ye not be judged." They were offended by the "moralism" of their conservative colleagues. Both sides called for moral guidance, but disagreed passionately about how and when it should be offered.

Halfway through the session, I noticed that many of the pastors were not participating in the debate at all. When pressed, they confessed that they were silent because they were uncertain about the pastor's role. Although the loudest participants—on the right and the left—were confident in their positions, the majority of the pastors were in the uncertain center. The disagreements of their colleagues made them even more hesitant. Though most agreed that adultery was wrong, they were unsure about what a pastor should say or do.

The pastors in this workshop are typical of many in our churches. Pastors confront ethical cases throughout the ministry of pastoral care, but are unsure about when and how to offer moral guidance. Many pastors today hesitate to make moral judgments at all for fear of giving offense, hurting someone's feelings, or becoming "judgmental." Many pastors are left in the "muddled middle"—uncertain about their role as moral guides. When pastors see the confusion of church and culture and recognize the limits of their own expertise, they shrink from the task. Yet when they witness the needs of church members and acknowledge their responsibilities as pastoral caregivers, they tentatively step forward and enter the moral struggle. This book is written for these tentative but bold pastors who want to become better, more responsible guides.

WHAT IS A MORAL GUIDE?

Morals

To understand the concept of moral guidance, we need to examine the words. What do the words "ethical" or "moral" mean? If you look up "ethics" in the dictionary you find something like this: "ethics—relating to morals." If you look up "morals" you read "concerned with ethics." These definitions do not overwhelm us with their precision. The words "ethics" and "morality" are often used interchangeably. Their roots do have a similar meaning. "Ethics" comes from the Greek word "ethos," and "morals" from the Latin word "mores" (Sykes 1976). Both words point to something that is characteristic of a particular people—its attitudes, customs, or beliefs about right and wrong, good and bad, virtue and vice. At this level, the task of the Christian as ethicist is simply to describe and reflect on those customs.

But if you have listened to ethical arguments on talk radio, at the barbershop, or around the dinner table, you know that Christian ethics is not simply about description. People are arguing with each other not so much about what is customarily done, but about what should be done. Ethical questions have a broad scope. What is good or bad? What is the character of a good person or community? How do we train people for virtue? What is happiness? These are sweeping questions. Ethics does not stop with controversial issues like abortion or sexual orientation. Our moral character is reflected not just in our decisions in a crisis, but also in daily life—in our use of money and time, in our treatment of other people, in the choices we make about work, or in hundreds of other daily activities.

For Christians, our decisions and character are shaped by faith. We are always both ethicists and theologians, because Christian moral reflection is interwoven with theology. We ask what is right or good, given our relationship to God and to each other. We learn to be moral in communities of faith. We are able to live according to the moral law because of the freeing power of God's grace experienced in these communities. Pastors, as leaders of congregations and preachers of the gospel, are crucial guides in these moral communities.

Guidance

What about the word "guidance"? The image of pastor as guide is not new. In contemporary and ancient pastoral care, "guidance" is a primary metaphor for the pastoral role (Clebsch and Jaekle 1964, 49–56; and Oden 1989b, 58–68). The word "guide" comes from an ancient Romanic word, "widare," which means "to know." The words "wise," "wisdom," "wit," and "guide" all share the same origin (Sykes 1976). Guidance presupposes knowledge and wisdom. A guide "shows the way" or offers counsel to others who are less experienced or less knowledgeable in a particular activity.

A guide knows something. And based on that knowledge, the guide is expected to lead and advise. A trail guide knows the best ways across a mountain. A white-water-rafting guide knows each turn of the river, the water conditions, and the capabilities of the rafters. A fishing guide knows which spots to fish according to the weather, the time of day, and what you hope to catch. In each case, guides share crucial knowledge with those in their care.

If, on a fishing trip, I asked my guide, "What bait do I use here to catch bass?" I would expect the guide to offer advice. I would be frustrated if he replied, "Hmm. So you're wondering what bait to use," or "What sort of bait do you feel you might want to use?" or, even worse, "Let's talk about your feelings about bait." And in that moment, I would not benefit from a complex lecture on the history of bait. I just want to know if I should use a "Lucky 13" or a night crawler. If, at a fork in the path, a knowledge-able trail guide asks the inexperienced group members to decide for themselves which way to go but refuses to tell them about the options ahead or to offer her own judgment about the two choices, the group would be disgusted. A guide who refuses to advise and share knowledge is no guide at all. A guide is expected to lead and advise.

One summer my husband and I traveled along the medieval pil-grimage route of Saint James across Northern Spain. Each year thou-sands of Christians make the journey by bike, on foot, or even by car. All are headed to the cathedral of Saint James in the city of Santiago de Compestelo. Guides have an important role on the pilgrimage. Some-times the trails are not clearly marked; if you are not careful you can lose your way. Occasionally the route splits and you have to decide which road to take. The path is dotted with hundreds of twelfth- and thirteenth-century churches, extraordinary bridges, medieval monas-teries, and charitable hostels. Without a good guide, you would not know enough to keep on the route or to find a place to sleep.

Most groups are led by guides who have traveled the route before. My husband and I relied on the expert guidance found in accounts of for-mer pilgrims. We read medieval and modern pilgrims' journals and studied maps. Most of the time the maps and journals provided more guidance than we could use. But sometimes, especially when things did not go as we had planned, we needed guidance in the form of a living person. We needed to talk to a guide who could help not just a generic pilgrim, but the two of us—with our particular problems, questions, and expectations.

One afternoon we spent several hours searching unsuccessfully for a small chapel famous for its carvings of the women at Christ's empty tomb. In the street we saw a guide waiting for her group to come out of a monastery cloister. I asked her if she could tell us how to get to the chapel. She said, "Well, hmm, I think, perhaps, if you wander around for a while, you may find it." This was hardly the guidance I was looking for. What sort of guide refuses to guide?

Good Guides

In ancient times and our time, good guides share distinctive characteristics and abilities. The church father Basil offered a list of virtues necessary to those Christian leaders "guiding" people "who are making their way toward God." The guide is to be "bearing witness by his own deeds to his love for God, familiar with the Holy Scripture . . . pleasing to God, a lover of the poor, mild, forgiving . . . not given to vacillation, [and] preferring God to every thing else" (Oden 1989b, 62). What are other characteristics of a good guide?

Good guides have distinctive knowledge and wisdom. They know the goals, the possible routes, and the dangers along the way. They know the people in their care, including their gifts, temptations, and desires. They are familiar with the terrain and with the necessary maps, tools, and techniques. Good guides know the customs and rules of the pilgrimage; they also know when these rules can be bent. Good guides know what to do when the normal plans do not work—when a bridge washes out or when a road is blocked. Good guides have distinctive knowledge.

Good guides are practiced pilgrims, constantly training and preparing themselves for their art. Excellent guides offer more than a checklist of technical advice; they have so fully internalized the technical rules and have so often practiced them that they have become second nature. Their discernment in a situation requires nuanced judgment that is as much like artistic perception as mechanical application. It is more like designing an original piece of furniture than rebuilding a carburetor.

Good guides are confident leaders. They are confident in their knowledge and are willing to share it with others. But more important than transmitting knowledge, good guides are able to inspire others, showing them a vision that will draw them toward the goal and reminding them of God's abundant grace that makes pilgrimage possible.

Good guides know their limits and temptations. They look out for their weaknesses and develop strategies to hold themselves and other guides accountable for their own limitations and weaknesses.

Good guides know when they need help, and they are willing to seek advice. They know when to share leadership and decision making. They establish relationships of mutual respect.

Good guides remember that others are free and responsible. Guides know that each person makes decisions. An individual might choose paths, fulfill obligations, or shirk responsibilities in the company of others, but he alone can make these decisions for himself. In most cases, pastors can guide but not coerce. People make their own decisions.

Good guides teach others the lessons of pilgrimage and guidance. They prepare themselves *and* their people for the journey. They not only pass along knowledge about the terrain and customs, but also help others find opportunities to put the knowledge into action and to become better pilgrims. They watch for critical teaching moments. They help form communities that will encourage and train their members.

Good guides develop excellent capacities for discernment. Guidance is especially needed to respond appropriately to people in their care. Good guides ask others about their talents and goals. They watch them, learning about their temptations, gifts, and potential. They know who has specialized training and who is a complete novice, who can be relied on and who is less trustworthy. Because of this knowledge, they are able to rely on those with particular expertise and to account for those with weaknesses and needs. Though good guides share leadership with others, they do not shirk their distinctive role as leader.

Good guides not only know the rules but also know that the rules must sometimes be bent and even changed. Guides must not only be familiar with the landscape, but also willing to do some landscaping. If customs are not fitting for the pilgrimage or seem tainted by human sin, then good guides, in prayer and conversation with other pilgrims, sometimes change them. If certain routes are less passable, then good guides may need to do some landscaping, changing the terrain or the social patterns. In this century, for example, we have made tremendous changes in the customary roles of women.

Good guides remember the most important things. While taking all of the techniques, customs, and skills into account, the most crucial things a guide keeps in mind are the shared destination and the source of power. For Christians, the ultimate destination, reached fully in eternity, is a life lived in love with God and others. Guides also remember the ultimate power. All guides are under the judgment and mercy of God, the Guide to guides.

The Limits and Possibilities of Guidance

The biggest weakness of the metaphor of guidance is that it underplays the uncertainty of our age. Does any one person know where we are going much less how to get there? How do guides account for disagreements about goals and paths? Admittedly, moral guidance is difficult and ambiguous; it requires greater sophistication than guidance given on a pilgrimage, a hike, or a fishing trip. (Fishing guides, pilgrims, and hiking fanatics might object.) Often we cannot know with certainty which choice is right. We disagree about ultimate goals. Obligations conflict. Rules are unclear. Older authorities seem no longer binding. Pastors trained as moral guides will never have full knowledge of moral right and wrong, and any claim that they did would make them the biggest fools of all. Moral certainty is not always possible in our tradition; indeed, being overly confident about moral judgment is often considered sin.

But just because moral guides cannot know everything with certainty, it does not follow that they know nothing. Through training and observation, pastors can become moral guides and can train others. Although the steps and strategies may be more clear-cut in other fields, a good moral guide shares a lot in common with other good guides. Good moral guides know about tradition, scripture, ethics, and theology. They know their people and themselves. They know the rules and goals of the pilgrimage. They know about the power, judgment, and grace of God. Guides know about sin and the tendency of humans, including religious leaders, to claim greater certainty than is possible. A guide also knows the opposite temptation—to abdicate responsibility and refuse to lead. A guide knows something; and based on that knowledge, including the knowledge of sin, the guide is expected to lead.

WHAT ARE THE TASKS OF PASTORAL MORAL GUIDANCE?

The tasks of pastoral moral guidance are many. The guide not only works in different settings (pastoral counseling office, classroom, and pulpit), but also fulfills different roles fitting to various settings, individuals, and contexts. What are the tasks of moral guidance in the ministry of pastoral care?

Moral Guides Are an Attentive, Active Presence

A primary task of moral guidance is to be with parishioners in crises. When church members struggle to discern the good, pastors can simply be present, listening and supporting. Pastors can help parishioners talk through the issues by asking leading questions and offering additional insights. Pastors can sometimes directly explain different ethical points of view.

For instance, a family in the hospital waiting room is trying to decide whether or not to have their grandmother, who is in the late stages of liver cancer, put on life support equipment. They are confused and ask the pastor or chaplain for help. The pastor could listen for clues about what issues are primary for parishioners. The pastor could explain some of the technical language and lay out a few crucial ethical distinctions. In this case, the pastor might explore different visions of medical care; for example, care can mean taking almost every technical, medical step possible and repeatedly reviving a terminally ill person. Care can also mean looking for fitting but less extensive treatments, alleviating pain and seeing to basic needs, but stopping short of extreme measures. Pastors can relate these options to faith—to our belief in the sacredness of earthly life and the good gift of eternal life. Though pastors may explain different points of view and offer their own faith perspective, they reassure the family of support. Pastors can serve as resources, drawing on the wisdom from Christian traditions and other fields such as medical ethics or secular psychology. The pastor is an attentive, active presence with the parishioner in crisis.

Moral Guides Are a Silent Presence or a Loving Absence

In some situations, pastors may discern that parishioners do not want guidance. In those cases, moral guides can be a silent presence or even a loving absence. The cue is taken from the parishioner. Except in extreme situations, such as child abuse or threat to life, forcing oneself into the situation is ineffective and disrespectful. On the other hand, the pastor could become overly cautious about moral guidance, hesitating to initiate or even to answer direct requests. Through practiced discernment, moral guides must judge when to engage in moral discussion and when to pull back. Such discernment is always difficult. The only thing certain about discernment is that moral guides are, on occasion, certain to be mistaken about it.

Moral Guides Lead By Example

Moral guides also lead by example. When I was in seminary, many of us resented the suggestion that pastors were to be models to congregations. We believed that no more should be expected of pastors than of any other Christian. At one level this claim is indisputable. We are all sinners redeemed by Christ and called to fulfill our responsibilities. And clearly the average congregation is stocked with dozens of people who are better models of virtue than their pastors. But even though all Christians should live responsibly and some of them do live responsibly, the consequences are more serious when pastors and other Christian leaders fall. Those who take on authority will be watched. Their misdeeds can ricochet in the lives of others. Chaucer, the great medieval storyteller, puts it this way, "For if the priest be foul, in whom we trust, What wonder if a layman yield to lust?" (Chaucer 1952).

A common claim in our tradition is that if pastors set poor examples and lead others astray, they bear responsibility not only for their own sins, but for the sins of others. The great preacher John Chrysostom was so reluctant to take on the burden of guidance and be ordained that he hid while his best friend was dragged off for ordination. (Ordination committees had extreme methods in those days.) He worried that in guiding others he might lead them astray. He wrote that he would rather "that a millstone should be hanged about his neck and that he should be sunk in the depth of the sea" (1984, 136). Leaders shoulder additional responsibilities and risks.

Of course, Christian guides are not "models" in the ordinary sense of the word. As a Christian, being a model does not mean being perfect or sinless. A good moral guide not only shows people how to live well but also how to sin well. A good guide can model confession, repentance, and openness to God's grace in the face of sin and failure.

Moral Guides Form Moral People and Communities

Moral guides not only respond in crisis, but also train Christians before crises start. Moral guidance must begin long before a difficult ethical dilemma is confronted. Moral guidance must begin long before an accountant is asked to fudge the numbers in the company's books or before a Christian is confronted with racial slurs. Moral guidance begins in Christian communities as we shape each other and hear stories of faith. It begins as we practice the values expressed in those stories and teach the ethical rules and goals of our traditions. Although moral guidance may find its most dramatic form in the hospital emergency room, it has its beginnings in the ordinary lessons of the Sunday school class-room and in the weekly experiences of worship. As we open ourselves to God's power in prayer and worship, we are transformed by grace. As we tell and practice the stories and virtues of our tradition, we are formed as moral persons.

Moral Guides Reform the Church

But moral guidance does not end with the transmission of our tradi-tions. Guidance is complicated, because we not only train Christians in the tradition, but also attempt to reform the tradition. We look critically at our tradition to see where it has not been true to its highest values. We also ask if there are central parts of our tradition that are not moral or holy. How do we respond to a tradition that has justified slavery, the hatred of non-Christians, the slaughter of Jews, and the denial of women's full humanity? As moral guides, how do we draw on our fallible traditions? When we talk today about sexual orientation, divorce, or women's rights, we are often uncertain about how to use our tradition. What happens when we disagree or when parts of the old guidebooks are questioned and a well-established path does not lead where we feel called to go? When may we amend the rules or engage in moral landscaping?

Moral Guides Transform the Culture

Christian moral guides face another challenge. We seek not only to reform our own traditions, but also to transform the wider public cul-ture. Faith shapes Christian opinions on the most controversial issues. On all sides of the debates over abortion, welfare reform, sexual orienta-tion, and capital punishment, we hear arguments from faith—argu-ments about our identity as humans, about our responsibilities and expectations for each other, and about who God is and what God expects. It is hard to speak of life-and-death issues without speaking of faith.

Debates about cloning are a good example. In these discussions, theo-logical issues are everywhere; we cannot take a step without tripping over them. We may begin with a discussion about a cloned sheep, but before long we are asking about ourselves, about what makes us distinctive, and about the limits of our technology. A Christian cannot talk long about cloning or most other public issues without running into theology. Given this reality, how do we Christians speak in public forums? How do we engage in public debate and help transform culture without selling our birthright or forcing our beliefs on others?

WHY PASTORS HESITATE TO GUIDE:
AN APOSTOLIC SUCCESSION OF RELUCTANCE

A new pastor called me looking for advice. A former grade-school teacher, Maria was the new pastor of two rural churches.[1] In a few hours she was scheduled to meet with a sixteen-year-old who was pregnant and had asked to talk with Maria about "what to do." The young woman was considering abortion. Maria was confident about the pastoral care skills she had learned in seminary. She knew how to listen with compassion, but she was unsure how to offer moral guidance. Not knowing what to say, she was tempted to "run away." She told me:

> This morning I was thinking that if I couldn't figure out what to say, maybe I should call my old principal to see about getting my teaching job back. I know how to teach first graders to read. But helping Christians live right is another thing. How can I guide confused people when I'm confused and when the whole church is confused? Lord, what have I gotten myself into?

Most pastors can sympathize with Maria. They look at the confusion and wonder how to guide. Whether pastors are in their fourth month or fortieth year of ordained ministry, they may sometimes wonder what they have gotten themselves into.

Gregory, a new pastor in his thirties, wrote that there was one task that had always seemed too difficult and "too high" for him—"the commission to guide and govern souls . . . especially in times like these, when a [person], seeing everyone rushing here and there in confusion, is content to flee . . . when the members are at war with one another and the slight remains of love which once existed have departed, and priest is a mere empty name." Gregory was so overcome by the confusion of his culture and the responsibilities of being a pastor that he ran away after his ordination at Christmastime. His people kept sending messages for him to come home. They needed him. By the time he returned to his church at Easter, the people were so mad, they would not come hear him preach. They refused to invite him to their homes and even declined his invitations.

So, in Eastertide of the year 362, Gregory Nazianzen wrote a letter telling his congregation why he had run away. He fled because the risks of guidance were high, the times were confused, and he was unqualified. He worried that if he led them the wrong way he would be responsible not only for himself, but for the souls in his care. Comparing the risks of the pastor to those of sailors who "cross the wide oceans and constantly contend with winds and waves," Gregory wrote that he preferred to "stay ashore and plow a short but pleasant furrow, saluting at a respectful distance the sea and its gains." In the end, he decided to come back to his people because they needed him and because the risks of disobeying God were surely higher than the risks of becoming a pastor. He was able to risk guidance because he trusted that he would be held and guided by God "Who is a Shepherd to shepherds and a Guide to guides" (1995, 221, 224, and 227).

Though Gregory and Maria are separated by ten thousand miles and sixteen centuries, they share a common reluctance—one familiar to pastors today. Like Maria and Gregory, pastors may hesitate when they see the confusion of church and culture. Many Christians disagree about what is right or wrong. And even when Christians agree about an issue, they are often uncertain about the role of pastors. Should pastors instruct, advise, or mind their own business? Pastors are faced with even greater disagreements in culture. Like Gregory, pastors may wonder how they can "guide souls" at a time when everyone is "rushing in confusion."

Pastors may hesitate because they worry that they will be poor models, leading others astray. An older Bishop warns that when pastors set a bad example, they are like shepherds who "foul the sheep's water with their feet" (Gregory the Great 1995, 2). Some pastors are reluctant to guide because they have seen others do it poorly. They know that self-righteousness and control can be hidden under the guise of pastoral guidance. Others may hesitate because of the distortions of Christian traditions. How do guides work with and transform our rich and checkered heritage?

Pastors may be reluctant because guiding humans is hard work. John Chrysostom compares the tasks of shepherding sheep and humans. What's the main difference? Humans are more trouble. If sheep tend to wander off, you can tie them down. Parishioners expect different treatment. You cannot bind them (no matter how tempting it might be). They are made "better not by force but by persuasion" (1984, 56). Guidance is also hard because each person is distinct. Feminists note that different people sometimes need a different message. Early church leaders also varied their counsel to fit the characteristics of parishioners—proud or humble, happy or sad, slow or hasty (Gregory the Great 1995). Guidance takes excellent discernment and long practice.

Pastors may hesitate to take on a task for which they feel unprepared. For Chrysostom, asking someone unqualified to pastor is like asking a cobbler to lead an army. He felt no more qualified to be a pastor than to captain a ship. Indeed, if placed at the wheel, he would immediately leap into the ocean to keep from "sinking the ship" (1984, 77). Guidance requires preparation. As pastors worship, pray, practice charity, and confess sin, they prepare.

Pastors also prepare as they learn about ethics and pastoral care. The fields offer both rich resources and wide gaps. One problem in pastoral care is that many have actively resisted mixing moral guidance with care. They have rejected "moralism" (Hiltner 1949) and hesitated to advocate the role of pastor as moral guide.[2] Many pastoral care experts and caregivers are likely to affirm instead the norm of self-fulfillment. They assume that individuals must decide what brings happiness and fulfillment. A central assumption of this book is that a primary reliance on the values of individual happiness and self-fulfillment, without further moral guidance about what makes a person happy, is morally empty. Moreover, it stands in contradiction to centuries of Christian teaching. Christians have insisted that true happiness is found in loving and serving God and others.

Other pastoral caregivers try to be morally neutral when talking with parishioners. I believe that there is no neutral moral ground in any relationship of care, especially a Christian one. Any method chosen or strategy applied rests on moral assumptions. Those who claim that parishioners should decide for themselves without guidance and formation assume that solitary individuals are well suited to do ethics. This is a moral assumption, not a neutral one. Moreover, the claim to neutrality is not a Christian assumption.[3] Christianity has never been a strong proponent of moral neutrality and extreme individualism.

In the academic field of Christian ethics, pastors also confront problems. For example, few Christian ethicists apply their work to the tasks of pastoral care and counseling.[4] In both fields, then, pastors find resources and gaps. Pastors can turn to these fields to gain many necessary pieces for a practical model of Christian moral guidance. This book helps pastors fit the pieces together.

WHY PASTORS MUST GUIDE AND HOW THEY CAN GUIDE

The Need and Call

In spite of their hesitations, pastors are called to guide. Many people in our churches are perplexed when they face ethical dilemmas. And even when able to discern their moral responsibilities, they may find it hard to practice them. Humans often choose to fulfill immediate desires rather than long-term responsibilities. Some pastors respond to these problems by retreating from moral guidance. I believe, in spite of their retreat, that most pastors want to be effective guides and to help parishioners. And the truth is that many pastors do push through their reluctance and struggle to guide parishioners as best they can. They move ahead, but with fear and trembling. When they face the enormity of human tragedy and see the poverty of their abilities, they question and doubt. I believe that many pastors are haunted by the questions that haunt me. "Did I say the right thing?" "How might I teach so that we will come to live more faithfully?" "What can I do to prepare myself and my people for tomorrow's tragedy and the next difficult choice?"

The Limits

This book seeks to prepare pastors for tomorrow's tragedy and the next difficult choice. But I would be lying if I were to suggest that this book would stop the doubts and the questions. I would be lying if I were to claim that the tools offered here could generate certain answers to complex problems. I would be lying if I were even to hint that this book offers a foolproof system for moral discernment. It is by no means foolproof; it is not even pastor-proof or ethicist-proof.

There is no moral system that will give full certainty and eliminate doubts on all matters. That is not only a fact from everyday experience, it is a reality of Christian faith. As Christians, we believe that our knowledge is limited. We know that at any moment in a person's life, sin is often rampant and always possible. Guidance will always be tainted by sin. No tools or ethical maps can change these facts of life and theology. All maps are partial and always partly wrong; moral maps, including this one, reflect the limitations of human hands and stand under the judgment of God.

According to some critics, our sin and limitation might be reason enough to avoid moral guidance. "Surely," says this line of thinking, "hypocrites alone could acknowledge their confusion and sin in one moment only to try to guide others in the next. That's like the blind leading the blind." Maybe so. Perhaps moral guidance is like the blind leading the blind. But in a world without sight, who is left to lead the blind but the blind? For those who have been called to be pastors in a world without sight, there is no real choice but to lead and guide.

The Guidance, Judgment, and Mercy of God

In the end, the bold or foolish leap into guidance is possible not because of the pastor's abilities, or even because of the needs of the people, but because of God. Because God has called, pastors must lead. Because God guides, pastors trust that they will be guided as they guide others. God's revelation in creation and Scripture provides guideposts. God's revelation in Christ gives not only a model and teachings for moral life, but also pardon for sin and acceptance in the face of failure.

Moreover, because of God's grace, pastors are not "the blind leading the blind." With redemption in Christ, the blind are given sight. In many parts of life, blindness remains. Human knowledge is limited, human truth corrupt. Even so, the faithful are given the sight that comes with grace. This new sight allows Christians to risk failure and sin. Trusting in God's mercy, pastors even risk practicing moral guidance. But because of the certainty of God's judgment, the depth of human need, and the reality of sin, pastors take these risks seriously and approach their vocations as moral guides with tentative boldness. Like Gregory, the reluctant guide, pastors risk guidance because they trust in the one who is a "Guide to guides."

HOW TO FIND YOUR WAY THROUGH THIS BOOK: A MAP AND DIRECTIONS

This book is written for reluctant and tentatively bold moral guides. It offers simple tools to foster good moral guidance in pastoral care. Drawing on the images of guidance and pilgrimage, it leads the reader through the landscape of ethics. It lays out a simple, practical map designed for ordinary pastoral care situations, while also recognizing the complexity of Christian ethics. Any map, no matter how well it depicts the landscape, is always oversimplified.

The first half of chapter 1, "Perplexed but Not Driven to Despair," centers on the case of a troubled marriage to illustrate the options or families in Christian ethics. Where the first half of the chapter charts the complexity, the second half simplifies. Using practical cases, it offers a single map for moral guidance in the ministry of pastoral care. In chapter 2, "Being Doers of the Word," pastors learn practical steps for guidance both in crisis counseling and in long-term moral formation.

While the first chapters draw on dozens of cases from the broad sweep of ministry, chapters 3, 4, and 5 focus on three common problems and cases found in ordinary congregations. Chapter 3, "Good and Faithful Servants," explores work and vocation. Chapter 4, "I Am My Beloved's and My Beloved Is Mine," centers on marriage and divorce. The last chapter, "Keeping Watch Over the Shepherds by Day and Night," looks at the temptations faced by pastors, particularly the problem of sexual misconduct. The chapter closes with a reminder of the dangers of guidance. Moral guidance requires humble, tentative boldness.

HOW TO READ THIS BOOK:
GUIDANCE FOR GOURMETS, GRAZERS, AND THIEVES

I designed this book for two kinds of readers—the gourmet and the grazer. As I wrote, the optimist in me hoped that pastors would read *The Pastor as Moral Guide* straight through with no interruptions. Gourmet pastors would savor each page, note the points of agreement, and incorporate relevant insights into their ministries. But the realist in me knew that my hope was not firmly grounded. As the wife, daughter, and sister of pastors, and as an ordained minister myself, I know how most pastors read books—on the run, between meetings, and in a stolen quarter-hour at the end of a long day. In these short moments, many pastors graze, choosing from this chapter and that.

Those of you who are gourmet readers will follow your normal instinct and read the book through. Bless you. For the grazers, on the off-chance that you happen to be grazing on these pages, I have several suggestions. If you like immediate practical cases, you will find them throughout the book. Even so, chapters 2–5 may be a good place to start. Chapters 3–5 center completely on common pastoral care cases from the parish. And chapter 2 offers practical tools for application. If you are looking for resources on a specific problem, use the table of contents to go straight to the relevant case. My tempered hope is that you might eventually, bite by bite, graze your way through the whole book.

Finally, if you, whether grazer or gourmet, are now standing in the bookstore aisle, flipping through this book, and finding yourself tempted to steal it, I have a brief word of moral guidance for you. Before you do anything rash, please turn to page 33 for a remedial lesson on Christian teachings about property and theft. Then, do not steal this book.

DOES ONE SIZE FIT ALL?: A WORD ABOUT YOUR GUIDE

I recently bought some panty hose to which the manufacturers had attached the label "one size fits all." They lied. Unless the hose were designed to sag, piling up around my ankles and spilling over the tops of my shoes, this was a gross case of false advertising. They did not fit. One size rarely fits all. In some passages, it may sound as if I am fashioning a generic, one-size-fits-all Christian ethic. Do not believe it. Though I have tried at every turn to be faithful to the broad stream of Christian belief, this model is not for every Christian. Some radical Christians on the left will disagree with my reliance on certain rules from our traditions. They may claim that I have sold out to the past. Some radical Christians on the right will object when I criticize our traditions. They may insist that I have sold out to culture. I am confident that still others will come up with criticisms that I have not yet begun to imagine. (Perhaps the only radical groups guaranteed not to criticize this book are arch-fundamentalists and atheists. They will not criticize it, because they will not read it.)

While this model is not for everyone, it is well suited for pastors who want an ethical framework simple enough to use and teach in the parish. It is well suited for many pastors who find themselves in the center of theological debate, believing in the gospel and loving the church and our shared traditions, while also seeing the corruption of that church and the limits of those traditions.

This model is both fitting for many Christians and shaped by my own faith. As an evangelical Wesleyan, I believe that we humans are free, that we are all recipients of God's grace, that we act responsively with God, and that we can find guidelines for a moral life through God's revelation in Scripture, tradition, and experience. Reading liberation and feminist theologians, as well as Augustine, Luther, and Niebuhr, I have gained a suspicious eye, learning to look for sin and deception in any ethics or theology.

In short, this is a *realist* Christian ethic.[5] It is realistic in two senses. First, this ethic assumes that moral claims point to something real and that we humans have partial, limited access to moral truth through God's revelation. Second, this ethic is realistic (as opposed to idealistic) about human sin and limits. Because of this second realism, I am suspicious of all moral claims. Given our sin, the limits of our knowledge, and our talents at self-deception, how can we trust our moral claims?

So, on the one hand, my realism is "optimistic" about ethics. Moral truth exists and humans have limited access to it. On the other hand, it is "pessimistic" about human sin. All claims about moral truth are ultimately limited. Because of the first, optimistic sort of realism, I believe that books like this can and must be written. The truth matters. Because of the second, pessimistic sort of realism, I am suspicious of moral claims, and am therefore astonished to find myself writing such a book. If offering moral guidance is a dangerous, foolhardy business, then writing a guide for moral guides is surely all the more foolhardy. In the face of human foolishness, we do well to remember our limits and turn to the one who is "a Shepherd to shepherds and a Guide to guides" (Nazianzen 1995, 227).

1

PERPLEXED BUT NOT DRIVEN TO DESPAIR
Maps of the Moral Landscape

But we have this treasure in clay jars, so that it may be made clear that this extraordinary power belongs to God and does not come from us. We are afflicted in every way, but not crushed; perplexed, but not driven to despair.
—2 Corinthians 4:7-8

Karen wanted to do the right thing, if only she could figure out what the right thing was. Soon after their wedding, Karen began to wonder if her relationship with Larry was "normal." He was often distant and anxious. When she tried to draw him out with kind words, he withdrew further. Karen worried that she was somehow to blame. Her best friend assured her that most couples struggle through their first year. But Karen and Larry struggled beyond the first year. Eventually, Larry was diagnosed with an anxiety disorder. Medication and therapy curbed the extreme anxiety, but Larry's psychiatrist admitted that a "full cure" was unlikely. They began marriage counseling to learn how to cope with his illness.

Karen was relieved to have a diagnosis and coping strategies. She realized that they had a lot to build on—a strong friendship, shared interests, and a common faith. When she started individual therapy, her counselor encouraged her to focus more on her own needs and fulfillment. Karen began to wonder if she and Larry could find greater fulfillment apart. Soon, Larry's disorder worsened. Imagining the struggle before her, Karen became depressed. But instead of isolating herself, she talked with others—asking for moral guidance about divorce. The conversations only amplified her confusion. While pastors and friends listened and offered support, they expressed deeply conflicting beliefs.

Karen's senior pastor listened carefully. After determining that there was no abuse or adultery, he gently reminded Karen of the scriptural prohibition against divorce. Faithfulness is found in obedience to God's Word. Over coffee the next week, the associate pastor acknowledged the depth of Karen's pain. When Karen asked, "What should I do?" the associate responded, "What do you feel you should do?" Pushed for advice, the associate refused to give it, insisting that Karen must decide for herself.

Karen also talked with the women in her family over coffee. Her mother counseled her to accept the sufferings of her marriage as a part of the Christian path to maturity. Karen's sister disagreed. As a Christian feminist, she insisted that the call to sacrifice was often a tool of the strong to control the weak. Karen's needs and fulfillment should come first, even if that meant divorce. Dismayed by the mere mention of divorce, Karen's grandmother redirected the conversation, assuring Karen that if she trusted in the Lord and listened for the voice of his Spirit, her marriage would be healed. No one contradicted the matriarch, but neither did they believe her. On hearing of this conversation, a friend counseled, "Just look into your heart to find what's right for you." After looking into her heart, talking with others, and listening for the Spirit, Karen was still confused.

I first heard this story from Karen. She not only understood the varying perspectives offered by her family and pastors, but also had been shaped by them. She could obey laws of Scripture prohibiting divorce. She could focus on her own self-fulfillment as the goal, asking if marriage would be best for her happiness. She could embrace suffering as a path to spiritual growth. She could question the social expectations of marriage from within a feminist or 12-step perspective. She could even listen for that internal voice. But she could not do all those things at once. From within and without, Karen heard only dissonance.

As I listened to Karen, I realized that her story reflected the tensions that many Christians face as they try to live faithfully in a pluralistic culture and a multifaceted Christian tradition. We live after Babel; like the biblical people, we hear many voices, but find little common understanding. Like Gregory Nazianzen, we see the confusion and long to flee. The ethical perspectives that Karen faced represent common options in Christian ethics. How can Christians find their way?

A FIELD GUIDE TO MAPS OF THE MORAL LANDSCAPE: CHARTING THE CONFUSION

Before helping others navigate among the different options, pastors must understand them. Ethicists have mapped out the various types of ethics. These maps or systems of classification are simply tools for organizing the confusion and fostering understanding.

One common way to chart ethics is to highlight two main maps or families—rule ethics and goal ethics. Let me illustrate. Two pastors learned that serious charges of misconduct were being brought against a fellow pastor. The younger pastor asked his older colleague, "What is wrong with my generation? Why do we forsake our commitments?" The older pastor replied, "I'll tell you what's wrong. Your generation seeks to find happiness. My generation sought to do its duty."

If you ask people why an act is right or wrong, their answers usually fall into these two families of ethics. One family looks first for the duty to be fulfilled or rule to be obeyed. The other family first asks about the consequences for the highest human goal (the love of God, Christian discipleship, or ultimate happiness). The most common dividing line, then, is between the duty to obey the rules and the desire to pursue the highest goal.

The story of the two ministers reveals an old dispute between goal and rule ethicists. The older man criticizes the goal ethic of the younger generation for overvaluing personal happiness. Many goal ethicists charge that rule ethicists can be rigid. While these two families continue their brawl, others have started new families and turned to other maps. In the alternate models, the focus shifts from rules or goals, to God's activity, conscience, the witness of the Spirit, character, liberation, and care. For all their differences, the varying types of Christian ethics draw from one pool of resources. The four primary resources are Scripture, human experience, reason, and the church's continuing witness in tradition. Christians accept these classic resources of Christian ethics when they believe that God's will and/or the moral truth are somehow revealed within them.

The different maps or families of Christian ethics may draw on the same resources and tell the same stories of faith, but they take radically different shape. While rule ethicists focus on obedience to laws, and goal ethicists on following the highest good, responsibility ethicists ask how best to respond to God's activity. Sense ethicists rely on the internal voice of conscience or the Spirit. Character ethicists emphasize the formation of character in community through hearing and living the Christian story. Liberation ethicists ask what promotes fulfillment and liberation for all creation. Care ethicists focus on offering responsible care to others and self within the bonds of relationship. These families of ethics provide valuable resources for the ministry of pastoral care.

What Rule Should I Obey?

For rule ethicists, moral faithfulness means finding the appropriate rule or principle and obeying it. Consequences are secondary. Many Christians draw on Scripture or church tradition for rules and principles. They can be highly specific ("Thou shalt not steal") or more general (care for the vulnerable). This model is evident in the response of Karen's senior pastor, who emphasized the scriptural prohibition of divorce.

In the ministry of pastoral care, there are benefits and drawbacks to a rule ethic. On the positive side, rules foster clear boundaries about right and wrong. The rules themselves become moral guides, serving as guideposts in moral crises. Rules are not easily manipulated to serve the temptations of the moment. They are also normally blind to differences in status. The prohibition against theft applies as surely to a company's CEO as to its custodian. Of course, these "benefits" are not a central concern for rule ethicists, who believe a rule is right not because of its consequences, but because of God's command.

The downside of a rule ethic is that it can fall into legalism and rigidity. The disobedient can become paralyzed with guilt, and the righteous can become proud. Because God is often seen as judge, the turn to God's grace can also be difficult. Recognizing these drawbacks, theologians like Luther and Bonhoeffer reminded others that salvation comes not in obedience to law; indeed, law reveals sin. Only through simple trust in Christ is salvation possible. Obedience to law is a response of joyful gratitude to God.

Where Are We Going?

For goal ethicists, moral faithfulness means discovering and pursuing our highest human goals. The pastoral caregiver helps parishioners remember and move toward these goals. Recently many pastors have accepted therapeutic versions of this model, emphasizing the goals of individual happiness and self-fulfillment. While traditional versions of Christian goal ethics often insist that the ultimate goal is happiness, this ultimate happiness comes from loving and serving God and others. Two versions of goal ethics are evident in Karen's case. Her counselor promotes the goal of self-fulfillment, while her mother uplifts the goal of Christian maturity through sacrifice.

A goal ethic brings several benefits. It is dynamic and flexible, allowing Christians to follow the guidance of the Spirit or the peculiar needs of the situation. In pastoral care, this model can help people to relate the immediate moment to their highest goals and ultimate relationship to God. A goal ethic also brings obvious dangers. It can be overly optimistic about the human capacity to know and do the good. It may promote a dangerous perfectionism. People can also choose poor goals or even use good goals to justify immoral means.

Goal and rule ethics dominate most moral reflection today. Our culture is now in a conflict between proponents of extreme versions of rule and goal ethics. On the goal ethics side, common among many people in mainline churches, individual fulfillment is primary. On the rule ethics side, more common in conservative churches, strict obligation to a seemingly arbitrary assortment of rules takes precedence. And these two sides are deeply suspicious of the other, further polarizing in reaction. Our problem in America today is not simply that we are faced with two very different ethical maps, but that we often confront caricatures of these positions. We need a re-evaluation of both sides. We need goal ethics with worthy goals and a recognition of the need for rules and boundaries. We need rule ethics that remember that the rules can become idols and are ultimately important in service of a larger call to love God. Goal and rule ethics are not the only options. Five alternative maps—responsibility ethics, sense ethics, character ethics, liberation ethics, and care ethics—complement the two primary maps, offering helpful tools for the ministry of pastoral care.

Responsibility Ethics: What Is God Doing?

For responsibility ethicists, the first questions to ask when confronted with a moral dilemma are not about rules or goals but about human response to God's activity. Moral faithfulness means responding in every moment as if responding to God. Because the primary proponent of this model, H. Richard Niebuhr (1943 and 1963), emphasized God's mystery and transcendence, the specific, practical application of this God-centered ethic is unclear. We cannot say for sure exactly how God is acting on us. From Niebuhr's perspective, that is not a problem. Indeed, the problem is that we often claim too much about God and moral truth. If Karen talked with pastors from this family of ethics, they would probably begin with questions about how God is acting and how she might respond. Of course, she could not say much with certainty (or specificity) about how God is acting. The pastor as moral counselor finds here an antidote to pride and self-righteousness. Responsibility ethics prompts deep humility as pastors offer moral guidance to parishioners, always remembering the limits of any human claims and the greatness of God.

Sense Ethics: What Do We Sense from Moral Conscience or the Spirit?

Sense ethicists believe that humans can sense moral truth by listening to internal voices of conscience or the Spirit. Moral faithfulness means cultivating and living by these voices. Christians who abide by conscience believe that it is a gift of God to help humans know the good. Others rely on the witness of the Spirit, claiming that through prayer and spiritual attentiveness, Christians can discern what is right. Karen's grandmother encouraged her to listen for the voice of the Holy Spirit, her friend for the voice of conscience.

Because sense ethicists do not rely on external authorities, they often have an egalitarian bent. They also can encourage parishioners to pay attention to many events in ordinary life that could be a part of the leading of the Spirit. On the downside, it is difficult to account for disagreement. Humans listening to conscience or the Spirit often hear different moral answers. Moreover, Christians can sometimes confuse their desires with God's voice, justifying dubious moral choices with a divine "permission slip."

Character Ethics:
How Is Our Character Shaped by the Christian Story?

Character ethicists begin with character and identity. Stanley Hauerwas (1983 and 1988) charges that many Christian ethicists focus on moral dilemmas but forget the larger scope of Christian moral life. The main task of guidance is to form Christians in community by telling and living the Christian stories and virtues. Moral faithfulness comes as we form and live out our Christian character. The community, faithfully living the story, is the ultimate moral guide. Karen's problem, then, is not simply about the dilemma, but also about her character as a Christian and her relationship to the community and its stories.

The danger of this map is that it can promote a narrow definition of the Christian story. Also, a pastor might find it difficult to understand the ways that parishioners are formed by other stories within the culture. This model also offers corrections for Christian ethics. It reminds Christians that the moral life is not first about decisions but about being Christian. It challenges churches and guides to remember the importance of teaching, witness, and example for Christian formation.

Liberation Ethics: What Is Liberating?

For liberation theologians (Ruether 1983 and Gutiérrez 1973), fulfillment includes all parts of life for all people: bodily needs of food and shelter; political needs of self-government; social needs of companionship; and the need of salvation. They remind Christians of the human tendency to misuse ethics to hide self-interest and protect power. Christians within this model will examine ways of living and thinking, always looking for the distortions of self-interest, particularly by those in power. Some feminist liberation theologians talking with Karen, for example, might explore the ways that male privilege is evident in Christian ideas of marriage. Karen's sister is asking these sorts of questions. The drawback of some liberation models is that they can be overly confident about our human ability to achieve new social patterns and fulfillment, without taking into account the continuing dangers of self-deception and sin in the new society.

What Is Responsible Care?

Proponents of an ethic of care focus not on abstract ethical principles, but on responsible care within real human communities (Gilligan 1982). Moral faithfulness means discerning and taking steps to provide the most fitting care for others and self in actual, messy relationships. The primary values in this ethic are not justice or fairness, but compassion and care. The center of responsibility is not the autonomous self, but the self in community. If ethicists of care were talking with Karen, they would be less concerned to determine principles than to help her come to a responsible decision that showed compassionate care for herself and others. The ethics of care reminds pastors of the larger human networks in which ethical decisions are made. It can help pastors learn to be attentive to new factors. At the same time, ethicists of care can lose sight of the other side, the importance of autonomy, justice, and the rights of an individual—even an individual with whom one is not in relationship. At its best, the ethics of care incorporates both sides.

Reflections on the Ethical Maps

This brief survey of the families of Christian ethics reveals the conflicting options facing moral guides. Christian ethics does not offer one sure set of directions leading to the fool-proof application of guaranteed moral truths. No wonder Karen was confused! Perhaps we should not be surprised at the complexity. If we expect a perfect system of moral guidance, unanimously endorsed, with easy, 1-2-3 steps, we have forgotten what our tradition teaches about human sin and limitations. Moral guidance is a lot harder than following a recipe. It is less like making a microwave dinner or assembling a tricycle and more like making a judgment about beauty or excellence. It is less like a close reading of sheet music for a Sousa march and a lot more like improvisational jazz.

Yet those who make judgments about beauty and those who are masters of improvisational jazz are not left without resources and standards. Some judgments and some jazz performances are better than others. Masters of improvisation draw creatively from many sources, combining and transforming, repeating and reshaping in new ways. Good moral guidance is improvisational.

A SINGLE MAP FOR MORAL DISCERNMENT

In the comic strip "Calvin and Hobbes," the young Calvin explains his ethical system of classification. He tells Hobbes, "Some people are pragmatists, taking things as they come and making the best of the choices available. Some people are idealists, standing for principle and refusing to compromise. And some people just act on any whim that enters their heads." Hobbes says, "I wonder which you are?" Calvin replies, "I pragmatically turn my whims into principles."

The cartoonist must know a lot about Christian ethics and human nature. We aren't so different from Calvin. Like him, many of us draw something from each of the various models. For all the differences among the families of ethics, many Christians turn to all of them at one time or another. Indeed, the second half of this chapter lays out a single map for moral guidance that incorporates insights from the different families of ethics.

It's important to remember that we are like Calvin in a deeper way. Any ethical map, including a composite map like the one sketched below, runs grave risks. Like Calvin, humans can use any classification available to justify "whims." No human tool, no matter how clear or simple, no matter how earnest or well meant, can ever overcome the reality of human sin and pretense. We share Calvin's temptation to "pragmatically turn our whims into principles."

A CASE: FOR THE LOVE OF MONEY

When I was a girl, I loved money. Barely thirteen and weighing in at eighty-five pounds, I chased down an armed pickpocket to recover my wallet and the seven dollars and change tucked inside it. For nearly a decade, I walked through the world eyes lowered, scanning the ground for the bills lost to others and now waiting, expectantly, to be found by me. I longed for Sunday afternoons when the pastor let me hunt through the coins from the collection plates for old silver dimes, buffalo nickels, and wheat-back pennies to trade for. I never passed a vending machine without poking a finger in the coin-return slot. By day my will directed an all-out search for money; by night my dreams were infused with money in extravagant excess—coins poured from candy machines, and bills from the sky.

Headed back to the bus after a church youth trip to the Arkansas state fair when I was fourteen, I stuck my finger in the return coin slot of a Tom's snack machine; fantasy and reality met. Coins poured into my hands. I filled my pockets, stuffed coins into my high-tops, tossed away my caramel popcorn, and then watched in rapture as the coins flew into the empty cup. When the vending machine deluge ended, I was weighed down by seventy-three dollars and forty-five cents in blessed quarters, dimes, and nickels. My shoes clinked as I dragged them along. I meditated on my extraordinary good fortune—the fruit of a long search, the fulfillment of many dreams; I rejoiced.

My preacher heard about the windfall about five miles out from the Little Rock fairgrounds. He wandered down the aisle to the back of the bus where I was counting my loot, retelling the story of its miraculous appearance, and defending my right to keep it. (An earnest friend insisted that I must repent and return the cash immediately or else risk eternal damnation.) The pastor listened to the story, laughed at my enthusiasm, and engaged me in a playful conversation about my plans for the money. By the time the bus had crossed the Saline River, we had left behind the joking banter and had begun to talk—us and the half dozen other kids at the back of the bus—about Christian moral responsibility; about the principles of justice and respect for others; about money, work, and theft; about our human loves, temptations, and goals; and about God's expectations, love, and mercy.

I remember only fragments of the conversation; I cannot tell you any particular piece of advice the pastor gave on the bus trip home. But I cannot forget that he guided us through a serious conversation about the moral life. He presented us with questions we would not have thought to ask. He listened to our answers, and he responded with more questions and his own answers and those of other Christians. Before we knew what had hit us, the preacher had guided seven little rednecks into a passionate conversation about moral discernment. And a few days later, I regretfully restored the seventy-three dollars and forty-five cents to its rightful owner, Tom's Snack Machines Inc.

THE GUIDING QUESTIONS:
BASIC COMPONENTS OF MORAL DISCERNMENT

Though I do not remember the exact conversation on the bus trip home from the fair, I do know that we discussed fundamental questions about the moral life. Below I have condensed those questions into four questions crucial to moral guidance. These four guiding questions are essential components of Christian moral theology and discernment. We ask: (1) What is happening? (2) Who are we and where are we going? (3) What rules or principles should we live by and when can we make exceptions? (4) Who is God and what difference does it make?

What Is Happening?

Whether we face a decision in our own lives or guide a struggling parish-ioner, a crucial question is "What is happening?" This data-gathering step has a broad sweep. Our observation could include obvious or minor facts, influences, and relationships. There are hundreds of questions. Who are the main players? What are the central responsibilities? What socioeconomic factors are in play? Who will be hurt and helped by this decision? We remember and ask about God's presence and activity in the pastoral encounter and the person's life. This process of observation takes place constantly, even though we are not always conscious of it. But when we train ourselves to be attentive, we may see the problems in a dif-ferent light. We notice things we might otherwise have overlooked. Ask-ing these questions is simply a way of calling ourselves to attention about details that often go unnoticed.

This point is especially important for moral guidance in pastoral care, because much of the training in psychology and pastoral care has taught pastors to attend to a fairly specific range of factors such as feelings, internal processes, and childhood history, while giving less attention to more commonplace parts of human life such as work, class, race, or even ethics and theology. Though some in the field of pastoral care have recently given more attention to other social factors, many caregivers still look at cases in the parish with a more narrow focus. It takes conscious effort to remind ourselves to notice other factors.

Let me give you an example from another realm of experience. As a boy, my husband learned to identify bird songs. He still notices them. Most mornings as I lie in bed half dreaming, my husband takes a bird roll call. "There are the cardinals. . . . Did you hear that wren?" For sev-enteen years I have been "hearing" the bird roll call without paying much attention. But recently things changed. I decided that I could learn the bird songs. And after a few months of careful listening, I now have cardi-nals, wrens, and blue jays in my bird-song repertoire.

Here's the point: Now that I know those bird calls, I hear them every-where. My world is suddenly filled with blue jays, wrens, and cardinals. As near as I can tell, the bird populations have remained constant. According to the Texas Wildlife Commission, there has been no unusual blue jay influx. My hearing has not changed. And, again as near as I can tell, I am not imagining these bird calls. The only explanation that makes sense (short of a bird-specific delusion) is that those birds have been there all along; I just never paid attention. Only when I trained myself to identify specific calls did I hear them everywhere.

Moral guides must learn to attend. The capacity to overlook is a nec-essary part of our everyday world. In order to survive—to work, pray, or read—we have to filter out most sensory data. But now we need to remind ourselves to notice. The birds have been singing all along, but we don't hear until we train ourselves to hear. Pay attention. Learn what to watch and listen for. Make a game of it. Practice your skills of observation standing in line at the grocery store or walking across the hospital parking lot. Try to figure out all you can about a person or a family by what they have in their shopping cart or by the state of their car. Try to identify the nature of a relationship between two people by the way they interact with each other. What strengths do they bring to the relationship? Transfer those skills of observation from grocery store and parking lot into fellowship hall and counseling office. Ask yourself, What is happening? What am I overlooking?

Conscious attention offers guides a broader view of the landscape and fine-tunes the capacity to spot relevant, minute details. Through careful attention, pastors and parishioners may come to notice landmarks, roadblocks, alternative paths, or dangers that were otherwise overlooked. They see things they never noticed, like blue jays and wrens. And when caregivers see more of the landscape, they become better guides.

What does all this have to do with Tom's Snack Machines? Because my pastor knew about my life and the lives of those around me, he was better able to understand and guide. He knew that I loved money but also that I did not need it to avoid starvation. He knew that I was particularly taken with arguments about justice, so he appealed to them. Having a full range of "facts," he was a better guide.

Who Are We and Where Are We Going?

This is a crucial question in moral theology, because our ethics emerge from what we think about human nature—about our capabilities, limits, and goals. Although Christians often disagree about human nature, there are general points, central to our common heritage, with which many Christians agree. Common affirmations about our identity include the following: that each human being is a valuable child of God, made in God's image; that humans have basic bodily and social needs; that humans have freedom and consequently bear responsibility for their actions; that true happiness comes from loving God and others; that humans sin; and that humans are loved, judged, and redeemed by God.

The second part of this guiding question—"Where are we going?"—focuses on the ultimate direction of our lives and immediate consequences of any act. What is the highest goal of Christian life? Are our actions and desires directed toward that goal? What stands in the way?

Common Christian goals include love of God and neighbor, eternal peace, and the kingdom of God.

What are the pastoral implications of these common claims about human identity and goals? On the bus from the state fair, my pastor respected both me and the Tom's machine employee as children of God. He was concerned both about the immediate consequences of theft and the long-term influence of the incident and the conversation on my character. Karen's mother saw her struggle as an opportunity for growth. Karen's sister thought the marriage prevented her from meeting crucial needs of her human nature. A guide might lead the parishioner in a discussion by asking a series of questions. Who are we? What sort of person does the parishioner feel called to become? What answers does the church or the Christian tradition offer?

Though there are many ways to understand human nature and goals, outlined below are claims that are central to this model and that are especially relevant to moral guidance.

- We are valuable physical creatures, made in the image of God, who have basic needs for things such as food, health, rest, companionship, and love. When we fail to see these needs in ourselves and others or when we deny the worth of ourselves or others, we sin. Pastoral caregivers can remind parishioners about their own needs and the needs of others, always watching to balance what the parishioner is leaving out. If a parishioner focuses primarily on self-fulfillment and ignores the needs of family and the larger community, then the task of guidance is to help the parishioner remember the needs of others.
- We are free creatures who have the power to change and choose. We are not victims of our past, other people, or our feelings. Pastoral caregivers can watch for moments when parishioners forget that they are free and responsible and then gently remind them of their power to make choices for positive change. Pastors can offer gentle reminders and also phrase questions and statements in a way that emphasizes the person's responsibility.
- We are social creatures with irrevocable responsibilities to care for family, self, and society. Many moral laws of Christianity and Judaism relate to these responsibilities. Choices that ignore or deny these responsibilities are immoral. A crucial component of most moral guidance is to help parishioners discern and fulfill these responsibilities to family and society. One of the most difficult parts of moral guidance is reminding parishioners that many of these binding commitments are lifelong and take priority over immediate, personal happiness.

• We are spiritual creatures made for the goal of ultimate happiness. This happiness is found through faithful love of God and creation and the fulfillment of our responsibilities. Often, immediate suffering or unhappiness is unavoidable if we are to be responsible. Pastors can remind parishioners of this ultimate goal of human life and also help them see the futility of any attempts to find happiness through crass self-fulfillment. Pastors can help parishioners shape all the smaller goals of life in relation to the ultimate goals.

• We are sinful creatures who deny our freedom and that of others, fail to see our basic needs and those of others, choose irresponsibility to self and others, seek happiness through immediate personal fulfill-ment instead of love and responsibility, and try to justify or hide our own immorality. Because sin can take so many different forms, pas-toral caregiving requires nuanced discernment and response.

• We are God's creatures. In all of our existence, we are creatures judged, loved, redeemed, and sustained by God. This affirmation is the foundation of all pastoral care. Because of God's expectations and judgment, pastors take their tasks and the parishioner's moral ques-tions very seriously. Because of God's redeeming and sustaining power, parishioners and pastors are able to become more responsible and to find mercy in failure. Because of God's love, both pastor and parishioner can risk loving each other and living faithfully.

As pastors and parishioners think through these questions in con-versation with Scripture and other resources, they can see new insights relevant to the immediate moral dilemma and the larger task of moral formation. Reflecting on these questions, we can remember our ulti-mate value, the value of all other humans, and the goodness of creation. They can prompt us to attend to all levels of human needs, obligations, and sin. They can remind us of our ultimate Christian identity and goals.

What Rules and Principles Do We Follow and How Do We Make Exceptions?

Moral guidance also helps parishioners examine the relevant rules and principles of the Christian tradition. Christians have affirmed many spe-cific rules and broad principles. These have included the goodness of all creation; the value of all persons; the centrality of love (especially self-giving love); a call for justice and care for the vulnerable; the Golden Rule; specific rules against killing, lying, stealing, and so forth; and spe-cific injunctions to care for the weak, to love God and others, and to speak the truth. We give these rules and principles varying weight and make different exceptions. Most Christians ignore Hebraic laws about food preparation but honor the Ten Commandments. We disagree about which rules are binding for all time and which are limited to the ancient cultures in which they arose. Moreover, many Christians ask whether some of these principles reveal more about God's will or the distortions of human will. As we are aware of these rules and their critics, we are able to see the ethical problems of the parish more clearly.

When I was considering what to do with the money from the Tom's machine, my pastor and I knew and accepted the rule that we shouldn't steal other people's property. Likewise, because of the Christian presumption against divorce, Karen and her senior pastor were hesitant to choose divorce without exceptional reasons. Even for those of us who admit many exceptions, in most cases the rules still hold.

In Christian ethics you can't talk long about rules without running into exceptions. One way to explore exceptions to rules is to examine the just war tradition (Kennedy 1994, 436–42). Though many Christians have opposed war, they have still found reasons to go to war. These classic criteria about exceptions for just war can provide tools for other cases:

- *Is there just cause?* Only when life and well-being are at risk does one have just cause to ignore the normal presumption against war. The just cause rule could be used in other cases, such as a person considering divorce from an abusive spouse. According to many Protestants, if the lives of spouse or children were at stake because of the abuse, the abused spouse might have "just cause" for divorce.
- *Is it the last reasonable option available?* Have all other avenues (negotiation, threats, or embargoes) been tried? This rule can be used in other kinds of cases. If, for example, your child was critically ill and needed a drug that you couldn't afford, would you be justified to steal it? Only if theft is the last resort. Did you talk to the bank about a loan? Did you try a community fund-raiser? On the other hand, in the case of a woman in an abusive marriage with the threat of physical harm, the first and only option is to ensure her safety, even if that requires separation or divorce.
- *Is the good brought by the war proportional to or greater than the destruction that comes from the original injustice and the war?* Proportionality can be applied to other cases. If a woman has been beaten by her husband, a proportional response might be divorce, separation, or the violence necessary for self-defense.
- *The violence of war is to be directed only at soldiers and not innocents.* This criterion provides a way of thinking about consequences

for innocents in other cases. In a responsible decision about divorce, harm to children, clearly innocents, would have to be a primary consideration.

• *Do we have a reasonable hope for success?* If the goals cannot be achieved, then it is not worth the destruction. If you were considering the theft of the drug for your child, you might hesitate if the drug is locked up in a maximum-security vault. You are unlikely to succeed and might be killed. What would happen to your child then?

Of course, these criteria for exceptions are not without problems. Indeed, they can be (and have been) used to excuse brutality. They also fly in the face of statements by Christ about violence. (Given the checkered history of the just war tradition, I prefer to call it "justified sin." If we have to break the rules, let's not pretend it is something purer than it is.) But for all the criticism, the criteria work insofar as they help us muddle along. If you are looking for tools for making exceptions in a responsible way, they are as good as any option I have found.

Remember that these exceptions do not nullify the rules. Exceptions occur when two principles or rules conflict. Moreover, having rules for exceptional cases does not mean that we can excuse everything. Imagine, for example, that a pastor is standing in a bookstore, glancing over these words, fingering this book, and wanting to steal it. According to the rules most of us learned in Sunday school, stealing is wrong. Are there exceptional circumstances that would justify theft? Is there just cause? Does a person's life depend on the theft? Even in the unlikely event that the pastor could find just cause, we could still ask if this was the last resort. Have all other options been exhausted (like buying on credit)? It is impossible to come up with a good argument for stealing this book. The pastor is simply going to have to break down and buy it. There are, after all, a few moral absolutes in this world.

For all their problems, many of the rules—including rules about exceptions—have worked pretty well. With their help, we've managed to change, amend, and even delete. We muddle along. We keep most of them most of the time, because they work all right and because they are shorthand markers for the accumulated wisdom of the people of faith who came before us. In addition, some of us believe that some of the rules are commands of God.

Who Is God and What Differences Does It Make?

The beginning point of Christian ethics is God. We are called to moral discernment by God. We are able to discern because of God's revelation. Yet we recognize the limits of all of our claims in the face of God's power and transcendence. Even so, we are willing to risk discernment and error because of God's call and God's mercy. Christian ethicists often move from the following claims: that God's active presence as creator, redeemer, and sustainer makes Christian moral discernment possible and human failure redeemable; that God's otherness, power, and judgment stand over all humanity, all moral claims, and all sin; that injustices and distortions of this world are seen in the light of God's justice; that God is revealed in Scripture; and that God loves and is concerned for the welfare of humans and all creation.

What questions might guides ask? What are the theological assumptions of the tradition, person, and pastoral caregiver? What is God like? How is God active here and in the life of this person? How is God revealed as creator, judge, redeemer, and sustainer? Is the parishioner focused on one aspect of God's nature or activity while overlooking others? Has the parishioner or pastor so focused on grace as to forget judgment? Has he or she remembered God's revelation in Scripture while overlooking the internal witness of the Spirit? Pastoral caregivers can draw parishioners into reflection about their understanding of God and its relevance to their situation.

Although these reflections might be undertaken more fully outside of crisis and in the broader process of moral formation, they are also appropriate and even necessary in moral guidance through a dilemma. Indeed, we are able to risk guidance and discernment in a dilemma only when we ask those theological questions and remember who God is. Though we hesitate and fail, we remember and move ahead knowing that God calls, reveals, judges, and forgives. Moral guides tremble in the face of human distortions and divine judgment. Moral guides take on their responsibilities, pressing on by God's grace and through hope in God's mercy and love.

2

BEING DOERS OF THE WORD
Reading Maps
and Teaching Map Skills

But be doers of the word, and not merely hearers
who deceive themselves.

—James 1:22

Stan comes to his pastor to talk about "problems with the wife." Before long he confesses that he is having an affair. Stan, his mistress, and their spouses and young children are all church members. He tells the pastor, "I know it's wrong by the old rule books, but it's right in my heart." Stan plans to divorce and remarry after "everybody gets used to the idea." How might the pastor respond?

After a church meeting, a single mother, Bonnie, mentions that her seven-year-old son is having problems "adjusting" to her boyfriend. She worries that "they don't like each other too much." Because Bonnie wants to marry the man, she asks to talk with the pastor sometime about how she can help everybody to "get along like a family." She adds, "It just kills me to see my two men fighting like this." On further questioning, Bonnie admits that her son ended up with a black eye after a "wrestling match" with the boyfriend. She reassures the pastor, "I don't think he hit him on purpose. He wouldn't do something like that." Later the pastor learns that the boyfriend has been convicted for beating the child of a former girlfriend. He has children from a previous marriage that he does not support or visit. When Bonnie meets with the pastor, what should he say? In the meantime, what should he do?

PASTORAL CARE AND THE CRISIS OF RESPONSIBILITY

Every pastor works with people like these who face moral crisis. For all their emotional complexity, these problems are not ethically complicated. They don't require a complex ethical calculus or moral slide rule. In many cases, people have screwed up, are contemplating screwing up, or are seeking help to avoid screwing up. If the deed is done, they may be trying to soften the consequences of screwing up. Of course, pastors and other caregivers do run into complex moral questions. Many decisions in medical ethics, for example, require complicated ethical discernment.

Even so, many cases that come through the pastor's office are straight-forward—like the two stories above.

Let's be honest about Stan and Bonnie. Can we say much in their defense? What is Stan, a husband and father, doing committing adultery with the wife and mother of another family? How can he plan to leave his family after "everybody gets used to the idea?" If you wait a few months, people "get used to the idea" of new wallpaper in the kitchen or a new dog in the backyard, but not the loss of their family. This case does not require elaborate techniques of ethical discernment. A man and woman have abandoned their responsibilities to their families. No matter how much sympathy we might have for them, they have done wrong.

And what about Bonnie? Though many pastors would understand her desire for companionship, they would be disturbed by her decision to marry a man who had given her son a black eye and had abandoned and abused other children. They could be dumbfounded by her expecta-tion that they will "get along like a family." What kind of family is she used to? If she wants to get along like a family, she needs to be a respon-sible mother and say good-bye to the boyfriend.

These people are courting disaster for themselves and others in their care. In pursuit of their own immediate fulfillment, they have forsaken sacred responsibilities. Now they are tempted to deny, rationalize, or avoid. What do we say when people act like this? What do we say when we act like this? While I have not made their mistakes, I have royally messed up—neglecting my responsibilities, whining about conse-quences, and blaming others. You may have done it, too.

These stories are not unusual. The majority of ethical problems faced by pastors, both in their offices and in their own homes, involve failures of responsibility. Quite often, the ethical questions are clear. So are the answers. Married people have no business sleeping around. Parents should protect children from brutality.

Pastors have heard these stories before. These people are in churches. Indeed, they pastor churches. We know them. We are them. The point is not to damn us all to the fiery pit. The point is to be honest, note our fail-ure, and do better. The point is to take responsibility.

Pastoral Care and the Culture of Irresponsibility

Pastors and other Christian caregivers are not immune to the crisis of responsibility. Some have neglected their responsibilities to guide con-gregations and to hold other pastors accountable. Some mainline pastors are so hesitant to sound judgmental that they lean too far in the other direction. Granted, many pastors do shoulder the prophetic role for social problems. On racism, sexism, and classism, some pastors are not afraid to speak out. I am grateful.

But when it comes to responsibility in personal relationships, these same pastors turn and run. I know because I have seen it done and have done it myself. And other pastors who are quick to speak about personal morality have neglected the call to social justice. The hard truth is that many of us haven't had the spine to take on our responsibilities in the culture of irresponsibility. We've turned our backbones into wishbones—easily bent, good for whims and wishes but not much more, not strong enough to stand up to the failure of will in our culture, not strong enough to say no to the disintegration of the family, not strong enough to denounce the greed that consumes our society, and not strong enough to preach self-control in sexual relations or justice in race relations.

I believe that most parishioners who come to pastors with ethical crises are seeking guidance from the Christian faith. If they wanted a secular counselor, they could find one. The fact that the parishioner brings the issue to a Christian pastor demands the pastor's responsible involvement *as a Christian*.

The Serpent Made Me Do It: Blocks to Responsibility

If human responsibilities are so clear-cut, why do we neglect them? We sometimes choose not to fulfill them because we prefer to do wrong or because we fear the costs of doing right. This problem runs from ancient days to our day. It is as evident in the book of Genesis as in the *New York Times*. King David committed adultery with Bathsheba, Uriah's wife, because he wanted to. David and his generation were not the only ones to choose desire over right. Our culture knows the same theme. Country singer Tanya Tucker sings of a woman in an illicit love affair. "I may be wrong, but I don't want out/It's a little too late to do the right thing now."

Most of us have sung a similar song. What keeps us from leaving the wrong and doing the right? Maybe we would rather enjoy immediate pleasure than take on the costs of responsibility. We would rather go out drinking than stay home and change our child's diapers. Or perhaps we are frightened by the costs of doing right. We are afraid to speak out against injustice. We fail for ancient reasons—because of selfishness, selflessness, fear, or laziness.

We humans are good not only at being irresponsible, but also at failing to take responsibility for our irresponsibility. We not only sin, but also make excuses for ourselves. When God confronted Adam and Eve with the charge of disobedience, Adam blamed Eve and Eve blamed the serpent.

So, when we make excuses today, we find ourselves in good company—or at least in old and famous company. There is one big difference between us and Adam and Eve. We are light years ahead of them in the creativity of our excuses. Imagine if Adam and Eve had possessed our knowledge of popular psychology when they stood before the Almighty in the Garden of Eden. Confronted with the apple charge, Adam could have told God, "I took the apple because I have abandonment issues from that time on the seventh day when you went off and left me." Eve could have said, "I was the second-born and thus had to prove myself." They both could have added, "Because of our early, formative experiences, we have a lot of baggage to deal with. It's not easy being Adult Children of the Almighty."

Today we face the same temptations but simply have a more dazzling repertoire of excuses. This is not news to pastors. Many pastors hear excuses all the time. If they are anything like me, they even make up excuses for themselves. A common excuse these days is victimization. People blame their failure of responsibility on someone or something else—particularly parents or a childhood trauma. "I slept around because my father was distant and I was looking for affection and approval." "Because of the way my parents raised me, I don't like black people" (or Latinos or rednecks or Muslims or Pentecostals). The immorality of one generation never gives the next generation a license to sin. We are responsible for our choices.

It is also common to blame another person or circumstance in the present. "I wouldn't have gotten drunk if my plane hadn't been delayed because of the snowstorm." "I wouldn't have lied if the boss hadn't asked me why my report was late." Short of physical coercion, we are responsible for what we do. Adam wasn't cleared of responsibility because Eve gave him the apple. We see the same theme in country-and-western lyrics. "You'd make an angel want to cheat." Or "Whiskey made me stumble, the devil made me fall." It's much easier to absolve ourselves and blame another—even a supernatural other.

Children are also masters of the blame game. When I was a girl, anytime my cousins and I broke wind, we blamed an old hunting dog. It was a sad day when that dog died. We were faced with the choice of taking responsibility for our own bodily functions or coming up with a new alibi. We found ourselves another dog. When kids play these games, we laugh. When adults excuse more serious behaviors, we stop laughing.

Humans can turn failure of will into a disease or condition. They pathologize it and then don't take responsibility for what they have done. "I can't hold my temper because I'm a rage-aholic." "I didn't stand up to him because I'm codependent and have low self-esteem." Perhaps the person does have low self-esteem. But that sad fact doesn't excuse the failure to take responsibility. The truth is, one of the primary ways we get self-esteem is by doing right.

The heightened awareness of feelings brought by popular psychology offers a whole new repertoire of excuses. "I stole the money because I was feeling insecure." "I left my kids because I was scared of the responsibility." Never before has such great wrong been blamed on something so ephemeral. Feelings are real, but they don't excuse actions. A crucial step in maturity is learning to do right regardless of feelings. The human will can master feelings. And by God's grace, we can even come to want and feel what God would have us want and feel.

One of my favorite excuses is the temporary loss of will defense. Similar to temporary blindness, this condition involves a temporary loss of ability; in this case, the will vanishes. A thirteen-year-old picked up by the police for breaking into a gift shop gave me this explanation: "Well, I was, like, standing around and saw the window was open. One thing led to another and, like, the next thing I knew I was like standing inside eating a candy bar. It just, like, kind of happened. You know?"

No, I don't know. Short of being transported into the store by aliens, we don't "just, like, kind of happen" to find ourselves standing in a closed store eating chocolate-covered stolen merchandise. We enter. We see the candy. We take. We eat. Unless our wills just go out occasionally—poof!—like bad brakes, things don't "just, like, kind of happen." Short of absolute coercion, we choose them.

Humans also have a long history of disguising sin as virtue. A man explains why he abandoned his wife and children. "I left them because I couldn't bring myself to hurt my girlfriend." A woman rationalizes her decision to stop visiting her elderly mother. "I did things for others in an unhealthy, codependent way, and finally realized that I needed to take care of me. It wasn't right to go see her when it wasn't coming from my heart." She not only makes the neglect of her mother into a virtue, but also makes the virtue of charity into a vice. Care of the other becomes codependency. It's a good thing the Good Samaritan never heard about this version of moral virtue. If he had been coming from a lecture on the dangers of codependency when he saw the man in the ditch, the poor guy would still be lying there. These excuses illustrate the extraordinary human capacity to avoid the right and justify the wrong. When it comes to justifying immorality, we are unsurpassed. Human beings are excuse-making animals.

THE DISTINCTIVENESS OF MORAL GUIDANCE

Precisely because of these common blocks to responsibility, the style of moral guidance differs from the style associated with popular psychology and some pastoral counseling. It may take time and practice for pastors to get acclimated to the differences. Pastors need to think consciously about the adjustment, just as they would have to think about driving on the "wrong" side of the road if they vacationed in England. Without conscious awareness of the difference, it is easy to fall back unconsciously into familiar patterns.

One big difference is the place of feeling. In much popular psychology (and some pastoral counseling), persons are encouraged to express their feelings of that moment. In moral guidance, feelings can easily become a distraction from the primary moral question. If I have messed up, I may prefer to talk about how sad I am than about my mistakes and what I need to do to make things right. This turn to feelings can even be misused to justify irresponsibility. The person who blames spousal abuse on feeling hurt is sidestepping responsibility.

The point is not to devalue feelings. Pastoral care is possible because of the feelings of love, empathy, and trust between parishioner and pastor. And many counseling sessions can appropriately center on feelings. Even in moral guidance, listening for feelings can be helpful—for a while. But continual overemphasis on feeling distracts from responsibility.

Feelings can also mislead. For example, people in extreme moods, either of happiness or sadness, often have poor vision. Those newly in love are not known for the accuracy of their perceptions. Love is not only blind, it can't smell or hear too well, either. Our strongest feelings—our desires and angers—are often poor guides for the moral life. We desire things that aren't good for us or others.

Pastors and parishioners may need time to get used to the differences. If the parishioner has been in a feeling-centered therapy, the pastor may need to be explicit about the shift away from feelings. After talking through feelings, the pastor could change directions. She could say, "You've described your feelings of pain and sadness. This problem has hurt you deeply. We may need to come back to those feelings later. Right now let's shift to some of the ethical questions you've raised."

Considering the weight given to feelings, it isn't surprising that some popular psychology has a bias against abstract, rational thinking. In the cultural context of some self-help talk, it's no compliment when someone tells you that you are a rational, linear thinker. Being "in your head" is seen as a way of avoiding difficult issues. In some cases, that caution may be warranted. But in moral guidance, we also see the reverse side. Being too much in your feelings can be a distraction from central questions of right and wrong. One aid in moving to those ethical questions, particularly if they carry a big emotional load for the person, is to shift to a more abstract level of examination—at least for a while. Exploring the moral questions from a distance can sometimes give a clearer vision of judgment. Then it is crucial to return to the relevance for the person's life; otherwise, the abstraction can become as big a block to responsibility as a heavy emphasis on feeling.

Christian moral guidance also has a different focus. Where much popular psychology and pastoral counseling centers on the needs and growth of the person in counseling, moral guidance also has a wider focus on the person's responsibilities to community. The guide is just as concerned about how the parishioner's choices will affect others, particularly vulnerable others. Many Christians have believed that fulfilling responsibilities to others is not only right, it also leads to ultimate happiness.

Much popular psychology highlights the immediate problem and feelings. Moral guidance differs in its understanding of scale and time. Indeed, in moral guidance a key step is to place the people and moral questions into the largest context possible (their relationship to God) and also in the longest time frame possible (their relation to eternity). The focus is not only on the individual person and broader social relationships, but also on God. The focus is not only on the immediate moment with its consequences for immediate happiness, but also on eternity and the consequences for eternal happiness. The pastor helps the person see that everything brought to the counseling session—the problems, hopes, feelings, and fears—are all encompassed by God's love and God's time.

Another difference is that much popular psychology (and pastoral counseling) is not very directive. The counselor takes the cue from the client and is much less likely to have an explicit agenda for the person. The person sets the goals. Indeed, one text insists that if pastoral caregiving does have "an evangelistic, moralistic, or political agenda," it ultimately "deteriorates" into "exploitation and coercion" (Shelp 1994, 321). And in many cases, the moral goal of self-fulfillment is not even recognized as a moral goal.

Moral guidance is much more directive about process and goals. Because there is an immediate moral task to face, the guide can help the parishioner stay on track. In this sense, moral guidance looks a lot more like short-term, cognitive, and crisis counseling than longer-term therapies. Moral guidance can also be more directive about the goals themselves. In Christian guidance, it makes perfect sense to work toward goals that are Christian. The guide hopes that parishioners will make good decisions and that they will mature as disciples of Jesus Christ.

Because of the practical focus on goal setting and achievement, short-term therapies are especially helpful for moral guidance in crisis. Some of the suggestions below are drawn from solution-oriented brief therapies.[1] The big difference between these therapies and Christian moral guidance is that guidance makes no pretense of being morally neutral. While solution therapies work with whatever goals the clients bring, moral guidance explores and refashions the goals as well. In the Christian life, we do not choose our goals out of a hat. We find them in a book and in community. In moral guidance, then, we help people to set immediate goals that are in keeping with the ultimate Christian goal—to live in love with God and others. One crucial part of moral guidance is to foster responsibility and encourage people to do right—both in fulfilling responsibilities and owning up to mistakes.

FINDING PATHS THROUGH THE ROUGH TERRAIN: STEPS FOR MORAL GUIDANCE IN PASTORAL CARE

Remembering Basic Tools and Assumptions of Moral Guidance

When pastors counsel about moral issues, they can encourage Christian responsibility. In a discussion of the specific steps for counseling (outlined below) there are several fundamental things to remember about moral guidance in pastoral care.

• *Remember the words of Ella Fitzgerald: "T'aint what you do, it's the way that you do it."* Whatever you say or do as a guide, say it and do it with love and respect for the parishioner. As you choose techniques and counseling methods, recognize that the single most important factor in a fruitful relationship between counselor and client or pastor and parishioner is a relationship of genuine care and trust. The kind of therapy chosen or the techniques used are of secondary importance.

• *Remember (and remind the parishioner) that God's love and power pervade the counseling session and all of life—including the immediate moral problem.* God's Spirit is present. Be attentive. Pray.

• *Remember that they are coming to you for help as their pastor.* You have authority for them by virtue of your calling, training, and relationship with them. Take authority as a Christian pastor. But use it humbly, respectfully, and responsibly.

• *Remember that moral guidance and even judgment can be offered in love and generosity.* Mean-spiritedness and excessive criticism are never called for. In the seventh century, John Climacus warned about the damage that can be wrought by an angry, fault-finding pastor.

A fox in the company of hens is an unseemly sight, but nothing is more unseemly than an enraged shepherd. . . . See that you are not an exacting investigator of trifling sins, thus showing yourself not to be an imitator of God (Oden 1987, 12).

• *Remember that people in crisis are often confused.* Don't assume a high level of thinking. Help them see the primary features of the moral landscape and the main options in their situation. Keep it simple.

• *Remember that some parishioners do not have the technical tools necessary for more complex moral discernment.* Pastors can teach ethical tools. At the same time, keep in mind that many ethical cases do not require complex ethical discernment.

• *Remember that even though persons in crisis may be confused and lack technical skills, they have tremendous internal resources.* As children of God, made in God's image, they have resources to know and do what is right. Guides help them learn how to find and use these resources.

• *Remember that even though pastors have authority and special training, the relationship of counseling is mutual.* Both sides bring problems. Both sides learn. And ultimately, parishioners, though helped and encouraged by others, make choices as individuals. Pastors offer information, guidance, and even a challenge, while recognizing the God-given freedom and integrity of individuals.

• *Remember that guidance does not mean coercion.* Unless the life or physical well-being of another person is at stake, the pastor should not force others into doing right. As John Chrysostom notes, it is much more difficult to shepherd people than sheep. If sheep tend to wander off, you can tie them up. If you "call more loudly," they will return. If sheep are sick, you are free to practice any treatment—"to bind them when it is necessary to use cautery or the knife, and to keep them shut up for a long time when that is the right thing." Parishioners are another matter. Parishioners are made "better not by force but by persuasion" (1984, 56).

• *Remember the serious consequences of the conversation for the parishioner.* Sometimes it may seem that the easiest course is to be neutral about their moral conflict. But remember the dangers (for them and you) of failing to hold people accountable. Characters, lives, and souls are at stake. On the other side, remember the dangers of pushing people too hard. It is easy to be demanding and then leave them with the consequences. When parishioners pay the price, be careful about running up their bill.

• *Remember the "universal rule of difference."* In moral guidance, as in any pastoral care, pastors deal with different kinds of people. In developing strategies, pastors should account for human variations. This was a common theme of guides in the fourth, fifth, and sixth centuries (Nazianzen 1995 and Gregory the Great 1995). The gentle need a different word than the angry. The timid do not need the same challenge as the proud. Learn to read people and adjust accordingly. Gregory Nazianzen compared finding the right balance for the needs of different parishioners to walking a tightrope. A pastor has to keep to the middle according to each situation, not leaning too much one way or another, to "guide them according to the methods of a pastoral care which is right and just and worthy of our true Shepherd" (1995, 212). The pastor is a tightrope walker.

Prompting a Straightforward Description of the Terrain: Reconnaissance

A first step in moral counseling is to engage parishioners in straightforward descriptions of the terrain. Pastors can simply ask parishioners about "what is going on." Through further leading questions, pastors can encourage parishioners to tell the full story. Remember to pay attention to the broad range of factors discussed in the guiding questions from chapter 1.

Hearing and Loving the Pilgrim

The most important step is to connect or establish a bond with parishioners. It is crucial not only that pastors listen to them and care for them, but also that parishioners *feel* heard and loved. Because moral guidance can be so difficult—touching on uncomfortable topics and challenging irresponsibility—it will not get far without a good relationship between pastor and parishioner. The best-case scenario is that the pastor and parishioner already have a relationship of love and trust. But whatever the previous relationship, the pastor must try consciously to connect with the person by listening and caring. Love has an extraordinary power to transform. The success of moral guidance and a good pastoral relationship depends on this bond of Christian love.

Asking Morally Leading Questions

Unlike many long-term therapies, the telling needs to move toward greater focus on the moral question. The pastor can ask leading, open-ended questions about moral responsibilities and options. If a young person has taken money from a candy machine, for example, the pastor could ask, "Who did the money belong to before you took it?" "What might the loss mean for that person?" These questions highlight the fact that the money did not belong to a machine but to another person. The pastor might follow up with questions like these, "What are your moral choices now?" "Okay, if you make that choice, what will this mean for the person who operates the candy machine?" These questions remind the teenager that she has a moral choice to make and that her decision matters in other people's lives. The pastor can also ask about the wisdom of Christian teaching. "What does our tradition or our church say about taking other people's money?"

If someone is having an affair (like Stan in the opening case), the pastor could ask, "Who is being affected or harmed by your decision to continue with the affair?" If the parishioner doesn't think anyone will be hurt, the pastor could ask about specific people. "What will this news mean for your teenage daughters (or your wife, your elderly parents, your Sunday school class, and so on)?" The pastor can follow up with a question about options. "What are the various options that face you now?" As the parishioner names options, the pastor can ask further questions about the unspoken options and the consequences of each option. "If you decide to leave your family, how might your decision affect their future?" The pastor could also ask about standards from the Christian tradition. "What is the teaching of our church on adultery and leaving your family?"

This shift to a moral discussion may take significant effort on the part of pastors, because parishioners resist. They sometimes do not want to face the wrong they have done and the hurt they have caused. If the person is highly confused or conflicted, for example, they may become obsessed with an incidental point or try to avoid the moral issue altogether. When humans do something wrong, they reveal extraordinary capacities for distracting and blaming. In moral guidance, the pastor can redirect the focus of the conversation by gently asking leading questions about parishioners' responsibilities and options.

Finding Overlooked Features

The pastor, through careful listening and discernment, also watches for overlooked or missing features. What factors go unspoken? The pastor could ask prompting questions to help the parishioner consider options or perspectives that may have gone unnoticed in the midst of the chaos. If Bonnie comes to talk with the pastor about marrying the man who has abused and neglected children, the pastor could ask her directly about the possibility of abuse. "If this man abuses your son, what impact will that have on your son's life?" By looking for these missing pieces, parishioner and pastor gain a more complete view of the terrain.

Uncovering Hidden Features

People may intentionally leave out crucial pieces of information because they are embarrassed or don't know how to bring up a touchy subject. They fail to mention the fact that they have a drinking problem. A young woman wants to tell her pastor that she is a lesbian, but is unsure how to broach the subject. If a pastor senses that the person might be avoiding something, then the pastor could ask, "Is there something you are leaving out?" or "Is there anything that you are hesitant or afraid to say?"

Looking for Ethical and Theological Landmarks

Watch also for key theological and ethical themes in the person's conversation. How does this person talk about God and morality? For example, do parishioners focus so much on God's grace that they seem to skip over questions of God's command and judgment? A pastor leaving his wife and children for a church member once told me, "God is a God of love who accepts me just as I am." In response, I asked him, "What does God expect of Christian fathers and husbands? What are our responsibilities to others around us who are also loved by God?" Remembering the "guiding questions" of the previous chapter, pastors can ask theological questions. "Where does God fit in here for you?" "What does God want us to become?"

Watch also for their implicit ethical model. Try to discern the ethical principles central to the case and the parishioner's life. Ask about other principles. Watch for clues about moral confusion or a clear bent toward one of the "families" of ethics discussed in chapter 1. For example, a woman came for counseling because she was upset that she had lost her job. She was fired when her boss discovered that she had lied about her past experience. The woman justified her actions saying that she had no choice but to lie because without the job she would have lost her new car. This person is operating out of a shortsighted version of a goal-centered ethic. The pastor could ask about larger goals of the Christian life that surpass the desire to keep a new car. The pastor could ask about rules and principles from the Christian tradition about telling the truth. In this way, pastors consciously look for and respond to ethical models used by parishioners.

Brush Clearing

Guides can also help parishioners clear away nonessentials. Together they engage in a kind of moral brush-clearing so that they can see the primary ethical issues and make out the main landmarks of the terrain. As I noted above, feelings are not a central part of moral guidance, because they can divert attention from the question of responsibility. So even though the pastor will listen and empathize with feelings for a while, the conversation may need to be redirected as a part of the brush clearing.

Other areas call for brush clearing, too. Out of anxiety or defensiveness, people may ignore their moral failure and focus instead on a minor issue or some small slight they have suffered. Others may be so petrified by an unlikely consequence that they talk of nothing else. The person may be working from an unrealistic fantasy. A teenage girl had to decide whether to be taken out of foster care and placed on the list for adoption. She decided to do it because she was convinced that she would be adopted by "Mr. and Mrs. John Elway." The only problem with this option was that the Elways knew nothing of her plan. It was total fantasy.

Some fears and dreams may be realistic but beside the point at the moment. A twenty-five-year-old woman considering abortion was distressed about what her decision would do to her turbulent relationship with her mother who lived 500 miles away. While that may be an important question, it isn't the focus of moral guidance. The pastor could say, "You are worried about how this will affect your relationship with your mother. For the moment, let's put that issue to the side and look at other questions you face." Pastors can shift discussion without negating the parishioner's feelings or anxieties.

Throughout these interactions, moral guides are looking for key ethical issues and factors. As conversations develop, guides even go fishing for other factors and options. By listening and questioning, guides and parishioners begin to see primary features of the moral terrain. The list of guiding questions and the families of ethics from the last chapter can be good tools.

Pointing Out Landmarks

When pastors recognize the primary issues, they can offer a summary that identifies key points and leaves out the extras hauled away in the brush clearing. This summary needs to be direct. It should emphasize the part the parishioner played in creating the ethical problem, that is, the choices she made that led her to the present situation. The summary should use plainspoken Christian moral language instead of the euphemisms of culture. Use the word "adultery" instead of "love affair" or the word "lie" instead of "stretching the truth." Assuming that the pastor and parishioner have established a good rapport, the pastor could say something like this:

> I want to make sure that I understand the ethical points of this situation you've been telling me about. You have chosen to commit adultery with a man who has prior responsibilities to his wife and children. You have very strong feelings for him. You don't want to give up this relationship, but you also don't want to continue to do wrong, particularly because of the pain you fear it will cause his children. You also mentioned that you worry about the impact at church if people found out that you were having sex with a married man. Are there other ethical factors?

Pointing Out Directions and Possible Paths

After summarizing the most relevant ethical points (including consequences and responsibilities), highlight the choice the person now faces. One approach is to ask her what choices she sees and then help her to fill out and explore the options and consequences. Often people forget that they are free and responsible. Remind them that they have a choice. Don't mince words, but also acknowledge the pain of the decision. In this case, the pastor could say:

> You face a tough decision—either to give up the adultery or to keep on with the adultery. Giving up the adultery will be hard because you want to be with him. Keeping on with it will be hard because you know it is wrong and because of the consequences to his family, the community, and your work with the youth group. Those are choices that I see. Do you see other choices?

If the question of right and wrong is pretty clear, then place the ethical question flatly before them as Christians. Many people know the right, even when they are doing wrong.

Assuming the Best

One way to approach this step is to assume that the parishioner has both the capacity to know the right and the desire, though perhaps submerged, to do the right. Using leading questions, the pastor may be able to remind the parishioner of something she already knows. The pastor could say, "Listening to you describe the situation and thinking about the fact that you came to see me, your pastor, I am wondering if perhaps you already know, deep down, what is the right thing to do. When you remember your best, most honorable self, what do you believe is the right thing to do as a Christian?"

If this doesn't get anywhere, the pastor could also use an imaginary case involving someone close to the parishioner. This exercise can get the parishioner out of the confusion of overwhelming feelings while still remaining personal and immediate. The pastor could ask her to imagine a similar case involving a good friend or a member of the church youth group. "If Gloria faced a similar decision, how would you advise her? What do you hope she would choose?" (See other exercises below.)

At some point in these interactions, the parishioner may say that it is right to quit the relationship. If that happens, the pastor affirms the choice and acknowledges the costs. "It sounds to me like you know what is right, that quitting the relationship is the right thing. I agree with you and so does our church. As hard as it must be, you've made a good and courageous choice."

Beginning to Walk the Path: Finding a Pilgrim Staff

Choosing the right and doing the right are two separate steps. How does a pastor help a person move from choice to action? The pastor could ask, "What are the first steps you can take immediately to do what is right?" After discussing these steps, the pastor could ask the parishioner to write them down. Together they could choose a few simple steps that the parishioner could do immediately. The pastor might also ask, "As you anticipate doing what you know is right, how can you find the strength to do it?" One way to get at this issue is to ask about past sources of strength. "In the past, when you had to do something hard, what did you do that helped you find strength?"

The pastor then reiterates the sources of strength. "So in the past you found strength to do the right thing by praying the Psalms and getting support from close friends. You also found strength by listening to your favorite music. You have good ways to find strength." If they need more reminders, ask them to think of other incidents where they found strength. Perhaps an athlete had to find strength to keep training. Or someone facing the illness or death of a loved one found strength to cope with her own grief and offer comfort to others. The point of these exercises is to help them find the strength to do what they have said they need to do. By making this thing—strength—something external, they can strategize about getting and using it. Pastors can offer direct affirmation, repeating the sources of strength several times during the conversation.

Giving Strengthening Exercises

Suggest homework that will help build strength. "In the next week, watch for the times when you find greater strength or when the fear isn't as bad. Notice what you are doing that helps build the strength. Practice doing those things. Ask yourself what other things you could do that would help you find strength." The goal is to help her become conscious of her power to find strength. With increased confidence, she will be better able to stop the adultery.

Offering Parting Words

At the end of the session, offer encouragement and reminders. Review the immediate actions planned and highlight the parishioner's strategies for finding strength to do right.

> You have chosen the right path. This may be one of the hardest things that you will ever do. I know that you can find the strength to break off the relationship. From what you've told me today, you have good resources that you've turned to in the past to build your strength. You listen to music, you pray, you sing strengthening songs. You are doing the right thing and you have good resources. I believe in you and know you can do it. More important, God is with you and loves you. You are not alone in this struggle.

Prayer is appropriate in most counseling sessions. Pastors can simply say, "Let's close with prayer." While this allows the parishioner an opportunity to object, pastors needn't wait for parishioners to ask to pray, nor must they ask for parishioners' permission. Whatever prayer is offered, a request for strength and guidance is appropriate. The pastor should take care to keep the prayer free from direct manipulation. Let the prayer be a prayer and not another device for summarizing the conversation.

Remembering Road Checks and Follow-Up Conversations

The pastor has a much better opportunity than most counselors for continuing to check in with people. Ask them how it is going. Remind them of their sources of strength. When appropriate, a follow-up letter reiterating the same points about finding strength can help. Make sure that the letter can be kept private.

WHEN SOMEONE CHOOSES A POOR PATH: RESPONDING TO "WRONG" ANSWERS

Some moral answers are better than others. A Christian who decides that it is right to lie for selfish gain or to expose children to abuse is simply wrong. Though we must carefully consider what we say to the person, there is no point in pretending that wrong is right. If a parishioner offers a "wrong" answer, what can the pastor say?

Finding Middle Ground between
False Neutrality and Harsh Judgment

In counseling parishioners dealing with moral dilemmas, pastors face several options. Some pastors have chosen a "false neutrality." This extreme (but very common) approach attempts to remain morally neutral and focus on what the parishioner wants to do or believes is right. The point is to help parishioners articulate their beliefs and desires. The trouble with this option is that the overwhelming consensus of Christian tradition insists that humans sometimes believe and want the wrong things. A pastor that stops with the parishioner's wants and beliefs is like a physician who settles for a patient's diagnosis and prescription—even if the patient's judgment is potentially harmful. If a patient is convinced that a heart attack is only indigestion, would a good doctor say nothing to convince the patient otherwise? Of course not. The good doctor would speak. The sick come to doctors and pastors for help and healing.

The other extreme chosen by some pastors is harsh judgment. This approach not only lacks the word of grace but also does not work all that well in counseling situations. It tends to stop discussion cold and alienate the parishioner. It is also hypocritical, because the pastor is a struggler and sinner. In addition, judgmental command does not serve a teaching role. If the pastor and parishioner can engage in a conversation where the parishioner is guided to a decision, the parishioner learns how to think and live ethically. Remember, however, that avoiding harsh judgment does not mean avoiding any judgment at all.

There is a wide middle ground between the pretense of moral neutrality and the extreme of harsh judgment. The best path will depend on the nature of the problem, the style of the pastor, the personality of the parishioner, and the quality of their relationship. What are some options?

Assuming the Best and Looking for It

One of the most effective options, even when someone has chosen wrong, is to assume the best of the parishioner. Assume not that they are right, but that somewhere within them they have the desire and the will to do right. This doesn't mean accepting a "wrong answer," but drawing out the "right answer" that is hidden within them. Martin Luther King, Jr. could appeal to the moral core of white racists because he believed that all people could discern moral truth and act justly. One way to draw out that hidden "right answer" is to "wonder" aloud if it is there. By using indirect, noncommittal language, the pastor might defuse a defensive reaction to the challenge. "You tell me that you don't think theft is wrong, but I wonder whether you are 100% sure about it or not. I'm wondering if maybe you came to me, your pastor, because there's a struggle inside of you. I don't know for sure, but I'm wondering if a part of you believes that stealing might be wrong."

Discussing Ethical Issues

In some cases, the pastor could shift to a more removed, intellectual discussion of the issue. Parishioners who like ideas or who are genuinely struggling with a difficult moral issue can benefit from a straightforward discussion of the different arguments. They could look at the options, talk about the guiding questions, ask what a rule ethicist or a liberation ethicist might say about the problem. If the issue is divorce, the pastor could ask questions and make direct statements about marriage and commitment. The pastor could ask why the person has chosen this course. These conversations can lead to new insights.

In some cases, the more abstract discussion can be unproductive. It can be a way of avoiding responsibility. Also, these discussions can stall or escalate into arguments. If they do escalate, it might be best to shift the conversation. An argument may simply alienate a parishioner and fuel a resolution to continue doing wrong. Because this is a counseling session and not an ethics debate, the main pastoral task is not to make the best argument, but to guide the parishioner toward a good decision.

There are other possibilities. Pastors could push the consequences of parishioners' choices in a direct and even confrontational manner. "Let me make sure I understand. You believe that the right thing, the moral thing to do as a Christian, is to choose to put your immediate pleasure and your relationship with your mistress above your commitment to your wife and children." Of course, this path could alienate the parishioner. Stating disagreement is appropriate and effective. Getting caught up in an explosive argument is not.

Assigning Homework

If the person is dug-in and defensive, one of the most effective paths may be to give the person some time to think about the questions. Pastors could give homework, asking the person to do several exercises over the week. Choose exercises that will work best with the parishioner. Are they close to a mentor or some children? If so, use their names. Have them view the situation from the perspective of old age.

> Imagine that twenty years from now your daughter Tammy will face a similar problem. How would you advise her? If your Uncle Elmo were still living, what might he think about this situation? Imagine that you are at the end of your life looking back to this time, what decision would you be proudest to see as a Christian? (See below for more exercises.)

Speaking a Difficult Word

Near the end of the session, the pastor could make a closing statement of disagreement that asks for no response from the parishioner. The tone of statement would depend on the personality of the parishioner and the nature of the relationship with the pastor. The statement can be honest and confrontational while still offering grace and encouraging the parishioner to choose the good. A pastor to Stan, the church member mentioned at the opening of this chapter, might say something like this:

> I want to say a few more words before we close. As your pastor, it's my responsibility to be honest with you. I believe what you are doing is wrong. You are shirking your responsibilities. Your choices and actions will be devastating for your family, especially for your children. This is not how God is calling you to live. I know you. I know that you are a good man and a good father. I know that you can draw on the best parts of yourself to do what's right and fulfill your responsibilities. I've seen you cross some

rough territory. You have the strength. I say this as someone who has sinned and who struggles every day with temptation. Often I fail. I know it's hard. But with God's help, we can do better.

Offering Continued Guidance and Care

Whatever is said earlier in the conversation, it is crucial that the pastoral caregiver close with a reminder of continuing support that offers grace but does not soft-pedal the sin or the consequences.

> This has been a tough conversation. We've talked about difficult issues, and I've been very direct with you. Before we close, I want to say one more thing. Whatever you choose to do, I will still be your pastor. I will love you. More important, nothing you can do or choose will lessen God's love for you. But surely God will be heartbroken, not only knowing your sin, but also knowing that somebody else—your children—will bear the consequences. But even in the face of this wrong, God's love never fails.

A SAMPLING OF TOOLS AND EXERCISES
FOR PILGRIMS AND GUIDES

Here are exercises to use in counseling or teaching when someone faces a difficult moral question and is hesitant or is making a poor choice. Use them and teach others to use them. Ask others to help make up additional exercises.

- *Use the bullhorn test.* Would you want this decision to be reported over a bullhorn at the high-school football game? "It's second down and eight yards to go. By the way, the Rev. Robert Morrison, there on the fifty-yard line, cheated on his income tax." Would it make a difference if your actions were broadcast over the loudspeaker at the grocery store? "Attention Foodland shoppers. Back at the deli we have a red-light special on pepperoni and over on aisle seven is Mindy Waterford, who lied to her parents about where she spent Saturday evening. Thank you for shopping at Foodland." (Kids like this exercise.)
- *Use the end-of-life test.* Imagine you are in your eighties. From the perspective of old age, what would you want to see when you look back over your life, particularly to this situation? Imagine yourself going through a life review in the last minute of life or the first minute of eternity. Is this decision something you will feel good about as a Christian?

• *Try the young-person test.* Would you advise your children, a young neighbor, or children from church to choose this course for themselves in the future? Would you want them to know that you had made this decision and to follow your model? Would it make a difference in your decision if they were sitting here now?

• *Combine the end-of-life and young-person tests.* Imagine yourself in old age. You are a person of honor, a Christian respected and loved by many. A younger person comes to you who faces a situation very much like what you face now. This person asks about your life and how you came through struggles. What would you say? How would this decision fit into that story?

• *Try the saint or good observer test.* Think of the two or three people of integrity that you admire most in the world. Would you want them to know that you had done this? How might they advise you? What would they do if they were in your place?

• *Ask about God.* Is this decision what God wills for your life? Will the decision draw you closer to God? Will it draw others closer to God? Will God rejoice? Will the angels and saints sing in thanksgiving?

• *Use the past-self test.* Look to yourself in the past. Remember a time when you were the most courageous that you have ever been. What would you have done then? How would that person see your present situation?

• *Use the future-self test.* Think about the person you would like to become as a Christian and the person that God is calling you to become. How would that person respond in this situation? Will this decision help you become the person that God is calling you to be?

• *Try the training test.* In this moment, you are training your character. Epictetus, the Stoic philosopher, believed that a person's character could benefit from facing a difficult challenge, just like a wrestler could benefit from training with a tough opponent. He wrote, "So when the crisis is upon you, remember that God, like a trainer of wrestlers, has matched you with a rough and stalwart antagonist.— 'To what end?' you ask. That you may prove the victor at the Great Games" (1909, 173). How is this decision training you? Will it make you a better person? Is this the habit you want to have form your character? Is this who you are? Is it who God wants you to be?

• *Try the global-population test.* Could you turn your decision into a rule for everyone around the world? Would you want those that you love most to live in a world run by this rule?

• *Use the vulnerable-loved-one test.* Think of the most vulnerable people that you love—an elderly relative, a toddler, a person with a serious illness or disability. Would you want them to live in a world run by this rule?

• *Try the jerk test.* Think about the most domineering, manipulative, and self-serving person you know. If you turned your decision into a rule for the whole world, how might this person use the new rule to serve self and harm others?

• *Count to ten.* Before doing something immoral, count to ten—not ten seconds, but ten days, ten months, ten years. Put the act on hold. Resisting temptation now will make you stronger and better able to make good choices later. If this doesn't work, keep counting.

STEPS FOR PRACTICAL APPLICATION IN THE PARISH: LONG–TERM MORAL FORMATION

Unfortunately, most moral guidance in crisis counseling is too little too late. Pastoral caregivers responding to crises have no choice but to do the best they can in a difficult situation. But how much better it would be if the church had done a good job of moral guidance all along the way. Then pastor and parishioner would "speak the same language" and be shaped by the same stories—even when they disagreed on some points. Good moral formation could offer better tools and a stronger character for facing temptation. Even when sin won out, the moral guidance of pastoral care in the crisis would be more fruitful if formation had started long before the crisis.

There are many ways to make the church a place of moral formation. Brainstorm with a Sunday school class, a committee, or a youth council. Here are a few ideas:

• *Tell the stories of Scripture.* Jesus' acts and words of kindness are extraordinary moral lessons. Tell about David's sins and righteousness. Tell about Deborah's virtues. Read the proclamations of the prophets. Tell the stories.

• *Tell about the transforming and saving power of Jesus Christ that redeems, forgives, regenerates, and makes it possible for us to live responsibly and to be forgiven when we fail.* Tell stories about that transforming power in particular lives—yours and others. Describe how this power helps people to live fully and responsibly.

• *Tell stories of later saints and sinners—both of Christian history and present.* People like to hear inspiring stories about the courageous. Children also like to hear stories about adults messing up when they were children, facing punishment, and learning to do right. Encourage people to tell their stories of moral struggle and victory in light of their faith.

• *Use the language of Christian morality in sermons, classrooms, and informal conversations.* Talk about the virtues. Lift up justice, courage, hope, and love. Speak the prophetic words of justice. Talk about sin, repentance, forgiveness, and new life.

• *Develop mentoring programs for youth.* Confirmation classes and youth seeker programs can be a great opportunity to link youth with responsible, faithful adults for conversation about the good Christian life.

• *Sponsor a workshop for parents on raising morally responsible children.* The church could offer different programs for various ages and issues. These classes might grow into ongoing discussion and support groups.

• *Start covenant or formation groups (or work with existing groups) to include moral questions in their conversations about discipleship.* They provide a network for moral reflection and accountability. Remember that the moral life is not only about personal responsibility but social responsibility as well.

• *Offer opportunities for parishioners (young and old) to do good works through a program such as Habitat for Humanity or a local soup kitchen or nursing home.* Nothing bolsters the moral life so thoroughly as the joy of doing good.

• *Remember the moral parts of worship.* Confession and forgiveness are moral acts. One moral goal of worship is to transform us and send us into the world as a transforming presence. Remember and build on these moral components of worship.

• *Preach forgiveness and second chances.* Knowing that all have sinned and fallen short of the glory of God, we preach not only about moral responsibility, but also about forgiveness and the power of God's grace.

• *Infant baptism, youth baptism, confirmation, and youth Sundays provide great opportunities to remind the congregation as a whole of its responsibility to set a moral example and live well before children and youth.* This is especially important for family members, close friends, and godparents at an infant baptism, but also for the whole congregation. When adults are baptized or become members, their preparation and follow-up training can include training in moral responsibility. These acts are also opportunities for entire congregations to renew their vows to live faithfully.

• *When a controversial ethical issue hits the news, briefly comment on it from a faith perspective.* In the Sunday sermon, newsletter, or classroom, pastors can simply make a side comment relating the issue to Christian understandings of God or creation.

• *In Sunday school classes, forums, and Bible studies, set aside time to talk about ethics.* Involve other communities of faith (churches, synagogues, mosques, and temples) in the planning and implementation of community-wide programs. Consider drawing on expertise among laypeople in church and community. For example, invite a physician to talk about end-of-life medical decisions and living wills.

• *Present ethical cases in Sunday school classes and youth groups.* People enjoy talking about ethics. Oprah learned that secret a long time ago. Ethical questions involve all the stuff of soap operas but with a sanctified spin. Although these discussions are often rowdy and fun, remember that some people may have had difficult experiences with the issue at hand. The tougher the issue was for them, the less likely they will be to say anything about it. Enjoy the discussion while also being sensitive to their feelings.

• *When teaching about ethics and ethical issues, be fair.* On disputed questions, present the various sides fairly. Talk about which positions are formed by Christian faith and how. Ask class members where they stand on the issue. Play it by ear when (and whether) to lay claim to a position. It is often best to explain the sides first. If you give your position too soon, the followers will be swayed because you believe it and the oppositionists will oppose it because you believe it. Either way, it kills the discussion. More important, it defeats one central purpose of these classes—to help people to think ethically and theologically as Christians. Even though they engage in this effort from within the larger tradition and in community, they have to learn to do it for themselves. This call for fairness and tolerance has theological roots. Out of respect for the integrity of others as God's creatures, made in God's image, we listen to them. Recognizing human limits, including our own, we know that we might be wrong and that we can learn from others.

• *When teaching about ethics, be theological.* The point of these discussions is to help people learn to think about the issues as Christians and to grow in discipleship. Use the language of faith. What difference does our faith make for how we think about suicide, racism, or cloning?

• *In preaching, talk about the Christian life of discipleship.* Tell the stories. Talk about the formation of character and about specific ethical issues. Don't only preach about virtue, but use illustrations that move people to strive for virtue. Inspire people to draw closer to God, to serve God in the world, to love others, and to live well. Remind people why we desire to be good and to live well—in gratitude to God. Inspire them to authentic gratitude.

FROM GUIDELINES TO APPLICATION: FROM PAPER TO LIFE

One Christmas, when I was a young girl, my parents gave me a banjo, complete with shoulder strap, finger picks, and a pamphlet covering the basic chords and bluegrass finger-picking patterns. Over the holidays I memorized and practiced. I ran through the finger-picking exercises every moment of every day. Any object could stand in as imaginary banjo strings—dashboard, dinner plate, pillow, and church pew. I learned those patterns not just by heart, but by ear, fingertip, and soul. I dreamed banjo picking. There was only one problem; my banjo pamphlet had plenty of chords and finger patterns—but no songs. After a week of constant practice, I did not know one song. I knew some of the technical components of banjo playing, but I did not know how to play banjo. At the beginning of the new year, my parents took action. Out of pity for me or just the pure delirium of listening every hour of every day to the ceaseless, twanging repetition of the same old chords and patterns, my mother bought a banjo book with songs. And she arranged for weekly lessons. It wasn't enough to memorize technical components of banjo playing; I needed to know how to use them. I needed models for good banjo playing and some guidance through the rough spots.

Moral guidance requires more than memorizing guiding questions, moral principles, or even rules for application. There is a big difference between learning about moral guidance and practicing it, between knowing about Christian virtues and helping others (and ourselves) learn to live by them. The next chapters apply these techniques and questions to practical cases. It is up to the reader to discern how to apply them in life. Remember the counsel from James, "Be doers of the word and not merely hearers" (1:22).

3

GOOD AND FAITHFUL SERVANTS
Making Money and
Finding Meaning in Work

What do mortals get from all the toil and strain with which they toil
under the sun? For all their days are full of pain, and their work is a vexation;
even at night their minds do not rest. This also is vanity. There is nothing better
for mortals than to eat and drink, and find enjoyment in their toil.
This also, I saw, is from the hand of God.
—Ecclesiastes 2:22-24

When Baltimore Orioles' shortstop Cal Ripkin broke Lou Gehrig's record for the most consecutive games played, Americans poured on the praise. The message was clear: In a culture that does not value hard work and reliability, we need models of hard work like Cal Ripkin. But for all his greatness, is Cal Ripkin the model we need for this culture? Is our problem that we don't work hard enough? The difficult part of this news story is that sloth is not the vice of the average American worker. We do have a work problem in this country, but for many the problem is often not under-work but overwork.[1]

We hear from the experts and see with our own eyes that we live in a work-obsessed culture. Many Americans are sacrificing basics like sleep and family meals to accomplish the work of home and business.[2] Professionals work longer hours to keep the jobs and standards of living they have. Blue-collar workers often hold down several jobs to support their families. On the other side, the poor struggle to find any work at all. As parishioners and pastors work longer hours, they try to balance obligations to employers, families, and communities. These hard choices between competing duties and goods are moral choices. They prompt questions about meaning. How does our work contribute to our communities and families? How does it relate to our faith in God?

Whether the issue is underemployment, overwork, or balancing family and job, adult parishioners struggle with work. Most Christians even bring their work to church on Sunday morning. Granted, parishioners don't keep laptop computers on the pews, fax machines in the hymnal racks, or washers and dryers along the outside aisles, but their work is still there. During sermon and song, prelude and postlude, people are not just thinking about Jesus. A businessperson considers the agenda for her Monday-morning staff meeting. A custodian working two jobs calculates how many extra hours he will need to work to cover the rent increase. A young father asks, "Did I put enough diapers in the bag before I took Timmy to the nursery?" A mother thinks, "While the kids are at youth group, maybe I'll have time to run to the grocery store." And, of course, the pastor is not only thinking about work; the pastor is working.

These mundane realities make a difference in ordinary parish life. Church members working eighty hours a week have little time to teach Sunday school or even attend worship. Working problems alter more than church attendance. They reach into all aspects of members' lives and, thus, the church's care. Working pressures affect many ordinary cases in pastoral care and counseling. Though some parishioners come to pastors with problems directly related to work, more often they are indirectly related. Marital conflict, general anxiety, and trouble with children are often linked to troubles at work. Working problems pervade the ministry of pastoral care.

WHEN WORK ISN'T WORKING:
STORIES FROM THE HOME FRONT

The Wests: Two Careers and One Hell-Raising Teenager

Rev. Cynthia Martin meets with the Wests, a couple in their forties who have three children. Brenda is a junior-high teacher and Mark a salesperson for an investment firm. They have asked for an appointment to talk about problems with their fourteen-year-old son Cody who is quick to give lip and slow to take responsibility. He has been fined twice for violating the city curfew, regularly disobeys the rules of the house, and is probably smoking marijuana. (They found the remains of a joint in his dresser.) Though they begin by talking about Cody, before long they are in an argument. Mark doesn't believe that the problems are as bad as Brenda describes. Except for a few incidents, Cody hasn't seemed particularly troubled to him. Brenda is furious at what she calls "Mark's indifference to Cody's problems." Predictably, the rest of the session is spent not on Cody's problems, but working through the conflict between Brenda and Mark. Near the end of the appointment, Pastor Martin says, "There are lots of unresolved tensions that we could discuss further— both about Cody and your marriage. I suggest that we meet again to talk about these issues and about the possibility of a referral to a marriage and family specialist."

Brenda and Mark nod, pull out their appointment books, and begin to look for a time. This exercise is the most revealing part of the session. Pastor Martin first suggests several late-afternoon times. Because Mark can't get off work early, they look at evening hours. That won't work, because Mark makes most of his sales at night. Pastor Martin offers to meet with them on Saturday afternoon, but that conflicts with their daughters' soccer games. Mark finally says that he could probably take off at 5:30 on Tuesday, two weeks from now—but he can't know for sure until the Friday before.

The pastor is no Sherlock Holmes, but has sufficient powers of observation to wonder if their problems are work-related. She asks them about their work schedules. Mark says that he has to work about eighty hours a week to make enough in commissions to keep up with the bills for their affluent lifestyle. Brenda works a little over forty hours a week as a teacher. Her "second shift," keeping their household running, adds another thirty hours or so.

When the pastor asks them how they manage, she gets a quick lesson in crisis time management. They found that they could live on less sleep and more microwave dinners than they had previously thought possible. They don't have family meals. They don't socialize much. As they rush off to their next appointments, the pastor mulls over the problems they face with Cody and their marriage. Pastor Martin believes that one important step for the Wests is to take a close look at the way they work. If they rarely even see each other, they can hardly help their son, much less strengthen their own marriage.

Debbie Pulaski: A Single Mother Sings the Overworked Blues

Brenda and Mark are not unusual. The average couple with young children works almost as hard. And this is not just a middle-class, couples problem. Poorer and working-class people, particularly single parents, often work double shifts and extra jobs just to pay the rent and buy food. Take, for example, Debbie Pulaski , a secretary and single parent of two. Debbie had been dragging around for months. All the things that Debbie normally looked forward to—outings with her kids, Sunday worship, and even her Tuesday-night bowling league—were a dull burden. When her family doctor advised her to seek counseling, Debbie turned to her minister. Pastor Will Schlauch listens to Debbie, asks her about the sadness, and offers a sympathetic response. They talk about depression and the "dark night of the soul." Hunting for overlooked factors, he also asks what else is going on in other parts of her life. As Pastor Schlauch begins to hear her story, he discovers that in addition to caring for her household and holding down a full-time job as a secretary, she has taken on another job that she can do at home on the weekends to save for her son's college tuition. And last month, when her mother spent a week in the hospital after surgery, Debbie lost sleep as she stayed by her mother's bedside each night. No wonder she is tired and depressed. While there could be other deeper psychological or biochemical issues, one obvious, though often overlooked, problem is that Debbie is stretched beyond her physical and emotional endurance. Keeping in mind Debbie's economic limits and family responsibilities, how can Pastor Schlauch respond?

The Williamses: Headaches and Homemaking

Single parents and two-career couples are not the only ones under pressure. Yolanda and Michael Williams have not been getting along lately. He is a small-business owner and she is a homemaker caring for their two preschool-age children. As the tensions of work and parenting have increased, so have their conflicts. They come to their pastor, Jimmy Rice, to talk about their problems and before long are rehashing ancient grievances. Yolanda complains that she never sees Michael. He in turn replies that no one appreciates the pressure he is under and the sacrifices he makes to provide for his family. Yolanda suggests that he is distant not because of work but because of the cold relationship he had with his father. Michael mutters that Yolanda has little room to talk because her mother is "a controlling witch." Through her tears, Yolanda tells her pastor, "He doesn't love me anymore. He never does anything with us. He's hardly ever home." With teeth clenched, Michael insists, "Don't be ridiculous. Of course I love you. That's why I work so hard. And what do I get? When I *do* come home I find a dirty house, screaming kids, no supper, and you on my back about not being home sooner." As they talk, other arguments break out; the air sizzles.

Pastor Rice considers asking about their families of origin, offering guidance on good communication skills, or recommending referral. Listening and weighing his options, he begins to shift the topic from their relationship to basic questions about their day-to-day life. Asking Michael about his work, he hears of the tremendous pressure Michael is under trying to keep his new business afloat. Working long hours, he believes, increases his chances of survival as a businessperson. When Yolanda talks about her average day at home, she describes an unending succession of diapers, laundry baskets, grocery lists, and insatiable children. She wants to keep taking care of their kids and the household full time. All she is asking from Michael, she insists, is "a little help with the kids and a few minutes of adult conversation." How should Pastor Rice guide them?

Bud: Lost Job, Lost Man

Not all work problems are about too much work. As Brother Sam Reagan greeted members at the door after worship service, Bud Cooper grabbed his pastor's hand, leaned in close to his ear, and whispered, "Preacher, they fired me last week. I don't know what to do. Pray for me." Before the pastor could respond, Bud was out the door and the next parishioner in line was shaking the pastor's hand.

Sam dropped by Bud's house the next evening—just about the time Bud usually worked in his garden. As they weeded around the squash and cucumbers, Brother Sam began to ask Bud about what had happened and how he was doing. Sam learned that Bud's job was eliminated when a new owner reorganized the factory. Sam could see that Bud was angry with his boss and scared that he wouldn't be able to pay his bills. Most of all, the unemployment had left him ashamed and lost. As Bud put it: "What am I without my job? Nothing. Nobody." How should Sam respond?

Pastors Reagan, Rice, Schlauch, and Martin all face common cases in the parish. For each household one of the major issues is work. How can these pastors guide parishioners as they explore their problems and think through options?

"THE OVERWORKED AMERICAN": WORKING PROBLEMS IN U.S. CULTURE AND PASTORAL CARE

Like the parishioners described above, many American workers are stretched to the breaking point. What problems do average workers face? Since the late 1940s, Americans have worked a little harder each decade. In fact, in the 1990s, average Americans work a month longer per year than they did in the 1970s (Schor 1992, 17–41). Employed parents with children at home have the highest hours—eighty-five to eighty-seven hours for mothers and sixty-six to seventy-six for fathers (Schor 1992, 21 and Ryken 1995, 45). Given all these extra hours, it is no surprise that Americans have more than doubled productivity and consumption since the 1940s (Schor 1992, 2). Many middle- and upper-income workers are suffering from an excess of the good life: "We've got it all. Now we just have to figure out how to fit it all into our closets and calendars. Our "day-timers" have run out of time. Our appointment books runneth over.

If Americans are working longer, where did those hours come from? There is no federal treasury of time that could crank out new hours in a shortage. Longer working hours create a time crunch. One casualty of the time crunch is leisure. Average Americans have 40 percent less free time than in the 1970s (Schor 1992, 22). They also have fewer hours for the basics. Average Americans get sixty to ninety minutes less sleep per night than they should (Schor 1992, 11). Meals suffer. The average work lunch "hour" is now down to thirty-seven minutes (Walljasper 1997, 46). Americans not only forgo long lunches, but also family meals. Twelve percent of working parents sit down for a meal with their children once a week or less. Working parents average just over three hours with their kids on work days (Bielski 1996, 27). The time squeeze has a tight grip and a long reach.

American workers face additional problems. With globalization, more jobs go overseas where labor is cheaper. As American businesses trim costs to compete, they cut wages and jobs. Those left are expected to work harder. With downsizing and job changes, competition can be fierce. The workplace begins to look more like a battle zone than a community of common purpose. The good news is that the unemployed will have a good chance of getting another job. The bad news is that the new jobs often pay half the wage of the old, and many are part-time with no benefits. All of these factors lead to high anxiety among workers. The poor are afraid they won't be able to survive. The middle class worry that they will fall behind and join the growing poverty rolls (Ehrenreich 1990). And those who have recently made it big, the nouveau riche, are holding on to everything they can. The nouveau riche don't want to become the nouveau poor.

These statistics and problems describe not faceless, generic Americans, but the particular Christians that fill our pews. The middle manager scared of losing his job is a church usher. The soccer mom who keeps up with her part-time job, the household, and the hectic schedule of three kids also teaches Sunday school. The Scout leader works two jobs at minimum wage and barely pays the minimal upkeep for his family of eight. The numbers include families like those described in the cases above. The numbers include a couple down the street from the church who work long hours at low pay and have not attended worship anywhere in years. The numbers are important for who they don't include. In a work-obsessed culture, how do we minister to those who, like Bud, *don't* work because they are unemployed, disabled, or retired? If our identities are tied to work, how do we value those who work less or not at all? The numbers also include pastors. In one study, 70 percent of clergy worked more than sixty hours each week and 85 percent were at home two or fewer evenings each week (Minirth et al. 1986, 83). The statistics about work represent millions of people, including those who sit in the pew, the pulpit chair, and the pastor's office. Work is a crucial issue for pastoral care, because it is a crucial issue for the people in the pastor's care.

WORKING ROOTS: A CHRISTIAN SURVEY

As we think about work, Christianity is an important voice, not only because many workers are Christian, but also because American models of work have Christian roots.[3] What do we find in our tradition? We see that God works. The creation story in Genesis describes God engaging in creative activity, making the world. God also works to maintain creation. In the beginning God worked. So did humans. In the second creation story of Genesis, we read that humans were created for work. God, seeing that "there was no one to till the ground (Gen. 2:5)," created Adam to "till it and keep it" (Gen. 2:15). In many other places in Scripture, work is seen as joy and virtue. It is a good task given by God. It can bring happiness and prosperity (Prov. 28:19). The writer of Ecclesiastes is not as convinced as the writer of Proverbs that hard work always yields prosperity. And even when it does, prosperity is itself subject to chance. It fades with time. Work is vanity. Yet, even in Ecclesiastes, it is what God has given us to do and brings pleasure. "There is nothing better for mortals than to . . . find enjoyment in their toil" (Eccles. 2:24). Our tradition has also claimed that work is toil and a punishment for sin. After the fall, God tells Adam, "Cursed is the ground because of you; in toil you shall eat of it all the days of your life" (Gen. 3:17). We see this theme in the story of Cain and in books like Ecclesiastes.

Some Christians talk about work as "calling." But in the Old Testament, a calling refers to a rare, exceptional task—like prophecy or kingship—to which God occasionally calls someone. In the New Testament, calling or vocation has a broader meaning. The believer is called to be a part of the body of Christ and to live faithfully. The New Testament does not glorify ordinary work. Of the few references, most emphasize the necessity of work to eat and give alms. This realistic appraisal points to its necessary place in survival and secondary place in Christian life.

The medieval church continued our tradition's ambivalence about work. On the one hand, work was viewed negatively as a punishment for sin and a distraction from higher things, such as the worship of God. But medieval Christians also had good things to say about work. It could be a remedy for idleness, restlessness, and lust; a form of penance; or even an avenue for contemplation of God. It was also necessary for food and almsgiving. Thomas Aquinas, a great lover of food, insisted, however, that it was better to pray than to work—just as long as there was plenty of food. Vocation or calling came to refer to the work of priests, monks, and nuns but not to "secular" work. This double standard defined medieval understandings of vocation.

Three factors joined to change ideas about "secular" work. First, the Renaissance highly valued the creative work of the individual. Second, intentional work became essential to fuel a new commercial economy. Third, Martin Luther and other reformers rejected the old "double standard" and insisted that vocation or calling included all work necessary to maintain society and creation. Each person, whether a cobbler, spouse, executioner, soldier, or priest, is called to work by God. For Luther, this was a general calling. God calls humans to do whatever work that is placed before them. Later in the 17th and 18th centuries we see a specific calling to a profession as doctor, teacher, or pastor. This focus on the individual having to discern God's call for a particular work, led to an "uneasy conscience" and a tremendous zeal for one's work.

With the growth of capitalism, perhaps spurred by this "Protestant Work Ethic," work came to have greater and greater value in the lives of individuals and communities. Eventually, though, many people, while keeping the high estimation of work, overlooked the divine purpose that had supported that high value in the first place. Increasingly, work and its immediate rewards of wealth and status came to be valued in and of themselves. For some, the Christian model of vocation was turned into a self-centered prosperity ethic. With the industrial revolution, hopes for the benefits brought by work were raised. As production and efficiency rose, many expected a higher standard of living and more leisure. Ironically, communism continued the high estimation of work. For all Marx's criticism of capitalism, he increased the value given to work, making it the central reality of human life and meaning. What Marx failed to account for was that capitalism and industrial economies could be partially corrected and that workers liked the benefits. For all the problems, capitalism and industrial technology did live up to some of the dreams. When experts predicted greater productivity and consumption, they were right. But when they predicted less work and more leisure, they were wrong. Industrial laborers worked longer hours than the agricultural counterparts of their own and previous generations. And though work hours decreased steadily from the 1800s into the 1940s, the trend then reversed itself.

In the last decades these work-related problems have increased. In the 1980s, known as the decade of greed, we witnessed tremendous profits for the very wealthy, but longer hours and lower pay for most workers. If the 1980s was the decade of greed, the 1990s is the decade of the squeeze. Time is to the 1990s what money was to the 1980s (Gibbs 1989). We obsess about it and want more, but while money can be made, saved, and leveraged, time is constant. We organize and regiment it, but the day yields no more hours, the year no more days.

This brief review offers insights into the daily challenges faced by pastors. Over centuries, people in our culture came to give ordinary work (not just church work) greater value. Eventually, the divine calling that supported that high value in the first place came to be neglected. At the same time, people came to expect more from work itself. They expected more products, better working conditions, and shorter hours. And for many, work did offer increased consumption, but often at the cost of consuming their lives. More work produced more things but did not provide meaning. When people looked for that meaning, many found that they had neglected the communities and practices that foster it. With more time at work, they had given less time to family, communities, church, and faith. It is no accident that the 1990s have witnessed a new interest in spirituality. This is a natural reaction to the greed and consumption of the 1980s and the time shortage and work glut of the 1990s. The spirituality boom emerges from a pervasive sense that something is wrong. Because the turn to spirituality often lacks direction (or goes in the wrong direction), pastoral caregivers have a responsibility to think about the problems as Christians and to guide parishioners who struggle. The current crisis of work and time is also a crisis of faith. How should moral guides respond?

WHAT'S OUR PROBLEM?: A WORKING THEOLOGY

Though Christians spend many hours working, we give the topic little coverage in sermons and pastoral care. Working problems have prompted best-sellers, but the church says little. Sure, we read the occasional article about pastoral care for those who have been fired (Culbertson 1994, 35–45 and Noyce 1987). Some Christian business organizations talk about evangelizing on the job. Others focus on not cheating or stealing at work. Guide books suggest that pastors mention work in sermons, visit the workplace, and read business magazines (Noyce 1987). But we hear very little about the role of the church in helping people think about the bigger issues. A Christian ethic of work must do more than promote evangelism or preach against deceit in the workplace. We need a fundamental reshaping of how we think about work and how we work. This is not just a problem for economists and social scientists. Our work patterns and models have theological and ethical implications. Our problem with work is that we value it too much and too little. We need greater idealism and greater realism about work. Let me explain.

Many Americans may recognize the high value placed on work by the Protestant Reformers. What is unfamiliar to many is the holy purpose in ordinary work. Many people have lost a sense of vocation. A fitting Christian response, then, is to raise the value of work by renewing our sense of vocation and reminding each other of the holy purposes of work (Fox 1994). But that isn't the whole story. In a culture that is work-obsessed, simply raising the value of work may be a deadly remedy. The push to value work was both the genius and sickness of capitalism. When pressed to its limits, it becomes idolatry. So, in addition to renewing the concept of vocation, we need to regain a new realism about work. If the first remedy is to raise the value of work, the second is to lower its value. Work is not only calling and joy but also toil and vanity. We often value work too highly, expecting too much of it, letting it consume not only our time but also our identities. Love of work can become idolatry.

What we need, then, is to lower the value of work. The purpose of work is survival and service. Our larger call is to be Christian. Employment is simply one part of that call. It is also difficult and subject to sin. And no matter what we achieve and produce, we hear the words of Ecclesiastes, "All is vanity." We need to lower our sights and recognize that all work has limited value. We aren't called to like it, just to do it. In short, we value work too much and too little. We expect too much of it when we look to it for ultimate meaning or when we forget that it is toil and vanity. Remembering God and the larger purposes of life, we are reminded of work's important but secondary role. We need a hopeful realism and a chastened idealism about work.

WHAT THEN SHALL WE DO?: A RETURN TO THE CASES

So, what does all this have to do with those harried, distressed people we met at the beginning of the chapter? How can we apply these reflections to their stories? For all their differences, each case reflects similar problems. Not only are these Christians caught up in typical contemporary problems (increased work, downsizing, fewer family and community supports), they also share similar assumptions. Like many other Americans they bring distorted contemporary notions about work, extremely high and unrealistic expectations of work, and a shortage of the theological and faith resources needed to respond as Christian disciples. How might their pastors guide? Though there are multiple problems and options in each case, here are a few things pastors might consider and suggest.

First, how can Pastor Cynthia Martin guide the Wests? Though the couple are worried primarily about their teenage son, it's likely that Cody is simply manifesting the symptoms of larger issues in the family and marriage. Whatever is going on, Brenda and Mark can't respond effectively if they don't take time to talk together and to be with their children. Among the many different issues, a crucial one is work. They have choices to make about their lives. After listening and asking questions, the pastor could place the moral problem before them.

You are faced with a common moral conflict. You have two good things that you are trying to balance. On one side, your work on the job is good and necessary. It helps you support your family and also gives meaning. On the other side, your work at home caring for the household and children is also good and necessary. Those are the two good things that I see, do you see others?

Pastor Martin can then ask them some questions about their choices.

This conflict and balancing act presents you with some moral questions and choices. First, I want you to think about how are you balancing these two moral goods right now. What are the consequences of the status quo for your family? Second, how, realistically, could you balance them differently? Could you find a balance that reflects what is most important to you as Christians? And if you changed the balance, what would the consequences be for the family, your job, your standard of living, and your egos?

Pastor Martin could also ask Mark and Brenda about immediate, practical steps. "What small things could you do this week that would make a difference?" Often a very small change can have a big ripple effect. Eating dinner as a family twice a week or reserving twenty minutes in the evenings to talk as a couple can make a tremendous difference. Pastor Martin could ask them to list a few small steps and then implement one or two at a time. The pastor could also ask about long-term choices they face and then pose a few big ethical questions about their lives.

I also want you to begin talking together about some bigger questions, about what's most important in your lives as Christians. Here's an exercise. Imagine yourselves as an elderly couple, talking together about your life. When you look back at your life as older Christians, what would you want to see? What would be most important as Christians? (For other exercises, see chapter 2.)

How might Debbie Pulaski's pastor respond when Debbie complains of depression? Pastor Schlauch considers several possibilities. Debbie could be depressed because of her difficult divorce. She could have chemical imbalances. Whatever the various issues, one problem is that she is simply overwhelmed by the demands of work on the job and at home. There may be a limit to how much these demands can change. She has fewer options than might a household with two working parents and more money. Her long work hours are necessary for the survival and flourishing of her family.

Given these limits, what can Pastor Schlauch do? Pastor Schlauch can listen to her troubles, acknowledge the difficulty, and encourage her—reminding her that she is doing a tough job well and that it won't last forever. We come from a tradition which knows that work is toil. He can also ask Debbie to think about two or three small things that she could do to make things a little easier. Perhaps she could arrange to have fifteen minutes to herself in the morning or get the kids to do the laundry. The pastor could suggest a few small steps to help with the depression. More sleep, exercise, a good diet, or even one minor change can ease depression. The pastor can also brainstorm with Debbie about potential sources of practical support from people in the congregation.

Finally, Debbie needs to take a look at bigger ethical questions about how she lives and how she relates to others. Perhaps the immediate problems she faces are unusual and will abate when her children are a little older (or even when she gets caught up on her sleep). On the other hand, if she has a long pattern of wearing herself out caring for others but never replenishing, she needs to reevaluate her life. Pastor Schlauch could guide Debbie to think about the place of service and health in Christian discipleship. They could talk about the importance of Debbie's basic needs within the context of her prior responsibilities to others.

How might Pastor Rice respond to Yolanda and Michael Williams? Whatever the different problems (issues with their families of origin or poor communication), one crucial issue is the reality of the overwhelming demands of a new small business and two preschool-age children. Simply hearing and acknowledging the problem, and assuring them that it is normal and temporary, can help. They have taken on tough responsibilities. Another important step is to look realistically at their options. Yolanda and Michael may face limited choices. Toddlers will not decrease their demands on request; and they do not do laundry. And short of giving up the business, their sole source of income, Michael won't be able to work more normal forty- or fifty-hour weeks for several years. Still, small practical steps and support from the church (as discussed with the other cases) could make a big difference. Pastor Rice could also begin a conversation now about the long-term choices they will face. He could ask them, "What is most important to you as Christians? How do you want to live as a family?" Even in the early stages of this conversation, Pastor Rice could ask them to think about one or two things they could do this month that would begin to change their future in keeping with this vision of their Christian life.

How can Brother Sam Reagan respond to Bud Cooper as he faces unemployment? There are at least three levels of care. First, Brother Sam can simply be present and listen as Bud talks about his anger and grief at being fired. He can also help Bud get connected with one or two other men in the church who have lost jobs. Second, Bud may want and need immediate, practical assistance. He may need a loan to buy groceries and keep the lights on next month. He may need help finding another job. Third, the most explicitly moral issue facing Bud is a theological question about his identity and sense of purpose. Although all the feelings of frustration and shame are a normal response to the loss, they are exacerbated by Bud's complete identification with his work. Without a job, he tells Sam, he is "nothing." He is lost. This is a problem. Making work the centerpiece of identity and life is idolatry. Eventually, in later conversations, Sam could begin to engage Bud in a conversation about the place of work in Christian discipleship. He could simply note the presence of these questions, saying, "Bud, as we've talked, I've sensed that you are struggling not only with the job loss, but also with bigger questions about who you are, about what is ultimately important, and about your faith in God." Sam could ask Bud how work relates to the rest of life and faith. In a few sentences, Sam could summarize his own theology of work. Through these conversations, the loss could become an opportunity for Sam and Bud to talk about what matters most in Bud's life and about how he can become a more faithful Christian.

STEPS FOR PRACTICAL APPLICATION IN THE PARISH

In light of these reflections, how can pastors and churches respond? Here are a few ideas.

Theology of Work

Remember what our tradition says about work. It is toil and joy. It is vanity and service to God and others.

Know your theology of work. How does it fit your practice of ministry—that is, the way you actually work? How might you change your practice to fit your theology?

Talk openly about work in preaching, teaching, and conversations. Name the problems. Ask members about their work.

Take authority on work issues—not to tell people what to do, but to guide. Encourage people to take a closer look—as Christians—at the ways that work and consumption affect their lives. Guide them to consider changing their patterns of work and consumption.

Read about American work habits, remembering that these statistics are true for Christians, too. Recommend books, articles, and tapes. Make them available.

Work in Pastoral Counseling

In counseling sessions, be attentive to the ways that work might play a part in the immediate situation. Remember that the statistics for the general population hold true for average counselees. Marital conflict, depression, and many other common problems can be related to work. Ask directly about work stress. Acknowledge that work is toil.

Take a work history as a part of your regular counseling routine with parishioners. Ask them about work—what they do, how many hours they spend, and what they like and believe about work. If you use a questionnaire in counseling, add questions about work.

In counseling sessions, don't just listen to work-related problems. Guide parishioners to reevaluate the way they think about work and how they actually work and consume.

In couples counseling, especially when the couples have two careers and/or young children, remember that work is often a primary point of contention. Loss of work can be a significant issue in couples counseling. Retirement and unemployment also create stresses on a marriage.

Include work issues in premarital counseling sessions. How do they understand their work for pay and their work at home? How will they divide responsibilities?

Recognize that some people are working hard not because they are work or consumption addicts, but because they don't have much choice (single parents, people with babies, and minimum-wage workers, for example).

Recognize that different people have different needs and problems related to their work. Some women in our culture are more likely to feel guilty about relationships being neglected. Some men are more likely to have self-esteem issues around work performance and more anxiety about promotions and firing. Also remember that all men and all women are not alike.

Pay special attention to the needs of those who recently lost work or retired. Check in with them. Also remember the grief of many parents when a child moves out of the house. This is also a work-related issue. Work-related losses often create personal crisis and are occasion for grief for many people. Name these issues and losses in preaching, worship, and conversation. Explore the possibility of forming different church- or community-wide support groups. Each of these groups (recently fired, retired, and so forth) brings different needs. Check with local mental-health agencies to see if such groups already exist in your community.

If possible, offer a temporary safety net and special care for out-of-work families. When families in poverty experience a job loss, they may not have enough money to buy food or pay for transportation to a job interview. Even many middle- and working-class families are only a paycheck or two away from poverty. Be aware of the concrete needs of the vulnerable. Watch for ripple effects throughout the family. Find out what services are available from community agencies.

Teaching, Preaching, Worship, Administration, and Transformation

In classrooms, sermons, and special programs, talk about Christian understandings of work and American work patterns. Guide parishioners to shape and live by Christian models of work.

Reexamine how meetings are scheduled and run. Be aware of overburdened lives when you plan church programs. Double-dip whenever possible, scheduling meetings with other programs. Watch out for meetings that cut into valuable family time (yours or theirs). Streamline church committees and assignments. What meetings are really needed? How can you best use busy and less-busy people?

Don't forget homemaking, which is often neglected in discussions of work.

Remember the importance of "Parents' Day Out" programs. They can provide a good breather for both mothers and fathers.

Talk with youth about work. Ask them what they plan to do, how they plan to work and why. Also recognize that they may now be overworked. Ask them to think about these issues in their families. Encourage them to give a year or more to volunteer Christian service.

Sponsor community forums on work. Make the church a center of public discussion on this important social topic and others. Move the church into the public square.

Work to transform work. Lobby for changes in the workplace and work laws. The major political parties have proposals for making the workplace easier on families.

Know yourself. Think about your work patterns and your theology of work. Are you overworked? How is work affecting your family?

Heal yourself. If you are guilty of devaluing work, do something about it. Model responsibility about work and overwork. Talk with family, colleagues, and staff about this issue.

Journal about work. Pray about work. Dream about how things might be different.

Get to work.

Remember the Sabbath.

Working Exercises

Here are a few questions that can be used in Sunday school classes or counseling sessions. They could be included in a newsletter, on the back of a Sunday bulletin, or in a pastoral care questionnaire. Ask parishioners to add to the list.

How much do you work each week both inside and outside the home? If you are married, how much does your spouse work? How do you share the household burdens fairly?

What do you like and dislike about your work? What do you hope to achieve with your work? What does it provide for your family and for society?

Do you think much about your work as a calling from God that serves God and others? Does your theology of work affect how you work or how you think about work? What is God calling you to do and be?

On a sheet of paper, rank the most important things in your life. Where does work fall? Now, on a separate sheet, list the things you spend the most time on. Do the lists match? What do you learn from the discrepancies?

Is there one small thing you could do to bring greater joy to your work? If possible, do it.

Is there one small thing you could do to bring greater joy to another person's work? If possible and appropriate, do it.

Think about a day when you enjoyed your work. What did you do on that day? Watch for moments when you do better at work and look for specific factors that make a difference. If possible, repeat the things that have made work better.

If you are employed, how would your perception of yourself change if you lost your job or took a lower-status job? Imagine yourself at a party where you know no one. Could you get through the evening without mentioning work? How would you feel if no one knew what work you did? Is your identity tied to your job?

Are you engaged in volunteer work in your community and church to serve others in need?

Do you honor the Sabbath and keep it holy? What do you love to do most on the Sabbath? Do you do it? How are you blocking yourself from Sabbath? If you are a pastor or other church employee who works on Sunday or a parent who works every day, when and how do you honor the Sabbath?

4

I AM MY BELOVED'S AND MY BELOVED IS MINE
Marriage and Divorce

Ah, dear God, marriage is . . . a gift of God, the sweetest, dearest, and the purest life . . . when it turns out well, though the very devil if it does not.
—Martin Luther[1]

"COULDN'T LOVE HAVE PICKED A BETTER PLACE TO DIE?"

By the time a marriage gets to the pastor's office for counseling, it's often on a downhill slide. Couples don't call the pastor when they are having great sex, but when they are having no sex—or, even worse, when one partner is having great sex with somebody other than the spouse. They make an appointment not to celebrate a marriage's growth, but to enlist help for its revival. They come not to say that love is flourishing but to mourn its passing and give it a "decent burial." After the angriest couple leaves the counseling office, a pastor may feel like humming the old song, "Couldn't love have picked a better place to die?"

When marriages crumble, pastoral caregivers are eyewitnesses to the destruction. They hear a tragic litany. "Preacher, we are filing for divorce." "My husband hit me." "My wife left me." Most pastors give the largest portion of their counseling time to these issues. One middle-aged Christian pastor complained about the rising rates of marital problems. "Nowadays one has more to do with marriage relations than with all other matters. Because of them we can hardly read, preach, or study" (Oden 1986, 113). In spite of his grumbling, the complainant, Martin Luther, managed to find time for other things. Many pastors today can affirm Luther's claim that marriage is "a gift of God, the sweetest, dearest, and the purest life . . . when it turns out well, though the very devil if it does not." Across continents and centuries, pastors know the seamier side of marriage.

CAN THESE MARRIAGES BE SAVED?:
ADULTERY, ABUSE, AND DIVORCE

"Nothing Will Stand Between Me and Happiness"

Linda Wilson asked the Rev. Tom Johnson, pastor of an affluent subur-
ban church, to meet for counseling about "getting through divorce."
Linda and David had been married for nineteen years and had two ado-
lescent daughters. From the outside, it looked like they had a good marriage and an abundant life. But Linda calmly explained that they had
been growing apart for years and now the marriage was no longer fulfilling. Deciding that divorce was "best for everyone," she was moving into
an apartment. Their daughters would stay with David because "their
school is nearby." She explained that David did not want to divorce and
had asked that they see Tom for counseling. Linda had agreed, not to save
the marriage but to "negotiate a friendly divorce." The purpose of the
preliminary meeting was to "explain the situation" and to schedule an
appointment for herself and David.

Well into the conversation, Linda admitted that she was "seeing someone else." Though this new relationship was "thrilling" and made her feel
"free and happy," she insisted that it was not the cause of the divorce. It
simply made her realize how "unhealthy and wrong" her marriage had
been all along. After scheduling the next appointment, Tom suggested
that she stop seeing the man—at least until she could work through
counseling with David. Linda's calm demeanor evaporated. Visibly
angry, she stood up to go, giving Tom a passionate discourse on love.
"Tom, most people will never know a love like this. It would be wrong to
deny it. No moralistic dogmas will stand between me and happiness." As
a moral guide, how should Tom respond?

"Stand by Your Man"

Pastor Judy Olsen received a late-night phone call. Margie, a parishioner,
had been beaten up again by her husband. After the last blows, Jack drove
away. Terrified of what might happen to her or her children when he
returned, she said that she couldn't "live like this anymore." Pastor Olsen,
who had heard Margie say the same thing last year after she and her old-
est child had been beaten, hoped this time would be different. On the
urging of her pastor, Margie agreed to contact a women's shelter immediately and then to call Pastor Olsen back to tell her that arrangements
had been made.

The next week Margie called to report that she was seeing a counselor from the shelter, studying for her high-school equivalency exam, and talking with a lawyer about a restraining order and divorce. A few weeks later, during the congregational prayers, Pastor Olsen was startled to hear Margie asking for guidance to be a better wife. After the service, Margie explained that she had gone back to Jack because he was "a good man deep down." "I am just going to learn to be a better wife. It may mean sacrifice, but that's my duty." Margie asked if she could drop by the office to talk about "building a Christian home." How might Pastor Olsen respond?

Returning to Karen and Larry

I had a counseling appointment with Karen, the woman described in chapter 1 who was considering divorce because of the tensions surrounding her husband Larry's anxiety disorder. Her therapist, associate pastor, sister, and friends had encouraged her to seek self-fulfillment. Her mother and senior pastor had advised her to fulfill her obligations. She was still uncertain. How should I have responded?

Pastors Johnson, Olsen, and Miles are guides in moral crises. These marriages present more than hurt feelings, poor communication styles, or old patterns from families of origin. The parishioners face tough moral decisions.

"Getting the Love You Want": Surveying the Landscape of U.S. Culture and Pastoral Care

Christian caregivers are moral guides in a vast landscape. Guides are called to consider not only the terrain of their Christian inheritance, but also of wider culture. As they examine social patterns, cultural assumptions, and prevailing Christian claims about marriage, what can pastors learn? How can they respond?

"Love American Style": Marriage and Divorce in U.S. Culture

American patterns of marriage and divorce offer a grim litany of statistics.[2] By conservative estimates, 16 percent of spouses have committed adultery. The 1948 Kinsey Report put the rates at 25 to 50 percent (Greeley 1994 and Michael et al. 1994). Fifty percent of all American marriages begun in the late '60s have already ended in divorce. We saw a 250 percent increase in divorce between 1960 and 1980. While divorce rose sharply, marriage rates declined by 30 percent and cohabitation rose by 600 percent (Gallagher 1996, 5). The effects of these shifts extend beyond the couple. Thirty percent of American children are born to unmarried mothers (Adelson 1996, 63 and Gallagher 1996, 5). (The rate nearly tripled in two decades.) Thirty-seven percent of American children are from divorced homes (Ehrenreich 1996, 80). Among the children who live with their mothers, a startling 40 percent have not seen their fathers in the past year (Galston 1996 and Waldman 1996, 37). And ten years after the divorce, two-thirds of the children have "virtually no contact with their fathers" (Gallagher 1996, 55).

Who Pays Out When Couples Split Up?: Consequences of Divorce

The consequences are even more troubling. In addition to economic loss (divorced mothers experience an average 30 percent drop in standard of living), health is also affected. Divorced men die at higher rates from heart disease and stroke. Divorced men and women are more likely to die from cancer (Galston 1996). Divorce is almost as deadly as chain-smoking cigarettes.

Respected studies depict the grim repercussions for children.[3] They experience two to five times the normal incidence of psychological problems, school drop-out, criminal activity, sexual promiscuity, and suicide. Children of divorce have five times the rate of school expulsion and suspension. They have lower rates of college attendance and employment. They marry at lower rates and divorce at higher rates. Children of divorce make up 80 percent of the adolescents in psychiatric hospitals, but only 12 to 15 percent of the enrollment in the nation's best universities. Adult women who are children of divorce have three times the rate of psychological problems. Divorce leaves a devastating wake (Powers 1997 and Zinsmeister 1997).

In spite of this devastation, only 20 percent of American adults polled in a 1994 survey believed that couples should try to make a marriage work "for the sake of the children" (Galston 1996). In contrast, youth are adamant opponents of divorce. A Gallup poll from the early 1990s showed that 75 percent of adolescents believe that divorce is "too easy." In another study, the only thing that junior-high students feared more than divorce was the death of a close family member (Zinsmeister 1997). For many, divorce may be more damaging than the death of a loved one (Gallagher 1996, 60–61). In one study, girls who lost their fathers to divorce had much higher rates of sexual promiscuity and self-esteem problems than did girls of intact families or those who lost their father through death (Zinsmeister 1997). Study after study recounts the devastation divorce brings for many children.

These statistics are sobering for anyone. For pastors, the numbers wear the names and faces of people in their care. In cases of adultery, abuse, divorce, and other marital problems, pastoral care always has ethical questions at the center. These cases are not simply emotional crises. They are crises of moral responsibility. Moral guidance is a crucial part of the ministry of pastoral care to marriages and families.

Second Thoughts About Marriage: What's Behind the Revolution?

Behind these statistics are revolutionary shifts in American ideas about marriage and divorce (Whitehead 1997; Gallagher 1996; and Bellah et al. 1985). Sociologist Robert Bellah contrasts the recent "therapeutic" model of marriage to the older "obligation" model. Where previous generations saw marriage as a social relationship bringing enduring obligations, many contemporary Americans define marriage as an expression of individual freedom and a path to self-fulfillment and growth. Therapy becomes "the model for a good relationship, so that what truly loving spouses or partners do for each other is much akin to what therapists do for their clients" (Bellah et al. 1985, 100). Barbara Whitehead claims that we have also redefined divorce as an avenue for growth and maturity (1997, 45–65). Several cultural critics (Whitehead 1997 and Gallagher 1996) argue that this shift has weakened marriage, encouraged divorce, and undermined moral responsibility, bringing devastating repercussions, particularly for children.

The dominant contemporary model, then, is marriage as a relationship for self-fulfillment and personal growth in which individual needs, benefits, and costs are weighed. This stands in contrast to an older model centered on obligation and responsibility (Bellah 1985 and Whitehead 1997). The new model is evident not only in popular magazines and self-help texts, but also in Christian books, both liberal and conservative. One popular book on marriage as a place to heal childhood wounds and find fulfillment bears a title that is a fitting motto for the self-fulfillment model: *Getting the Love You Want* (Hendrix 1988).

We see these themes in the cases above. Linda leaves her family because she finds greater "fulfillment" with her lover. Karen is confused by the conflicting messages of obligation and self-fulfillment. In these cases and others, good pastoral caregivers must consider the cultural patterns and ideas that shape parishioners. In addition, pastors are public theologians who help to reshape the ways we think about and practice marriage and divorce.

You Can't Always Get What You Want. Or Can You?: Ethics and Pastoral Care

Though the field of pastoral care is a great resource for ministers, it is of limited help as they try to challenge cultural models of marriage and divorce. The field of pastoral care has been heavily influenced by both secular psychology and popular cultural assumptions. Indeed, one reason that pastoral counselors may be so attracted to secular psychology is precisely because its values are easier to translate to our culture. As one pastoral care text puts it, "It is much easier for the psychological counselor to move Freud's Vienna to the United States than it is for the pastoral counselor to bring Paul's Corinth to America" (Stroup and Wood 1974, 3).

Many in the field of pastoral care claim that the purposes of marriage and sexuality center on self-fulfillment. For Seward Hiltner (1953, 177) social guidelines about sex are for the purpose of "the realization of personal and interpersonal values." For Herb Anderson (1984) marriage provides not only for social needs but also for individuation. For Harville Hendrix (1988), marriage is a place to heal childhood wounds. In these perspectives, a central purpose of marriage is individual fulfillment and growth.

This pattern is also evident when some pastoral care texts address divorce and adultery. Where Christian texts from earlier generations were unambiguous in their judgment of divorce and adultery, some recent books offer little or no judgment. This move is in keeping with the long tradition of rejecting "moralism" in pastoral care (Hiltner 1949).

According to one pastoral caregiver, even when a person is engaging in "high-risk" sexual practices, Christian caregivers should "offer pastoral care unconditioned by judgment" (Shelp 1994, 318). The "moral values and commitments" of the parishioner, while different from the caregiver, "deserve to be acknowledged and accepted because they represent that person's notion of the life worth living" (1994, 320). From this caregiver's perspective, while high-risk sexual behaviors can be morally "accepted," calling parishioners to accountability is "a morally questionable activity of exploitation and coercion" (1994, 319).

"High-risk behaviors" include sex with many partners and no condoms. Aside from other moral considerations, people who engage in such behaviors are morally irresponsible because they risk lives in pursuit of pleasure. In such cases, caregivers who fail to address moral issues are accomplices. The ministry of pastoral care cannot responsibly avoid moral judgment. Whether the problem is irresponsible sexual activity, domestic violence, or racism, pastors face evils that must be named and fought.

Some Christians not only shy away from judgment, but even claim that sexual practices like adultery can be moral. According to this argument, a primary Christian consideration in evaluating sexual activities is not fidelity, but "justice." "From a justice perspective, it is entirely fitting . . . to celebrate all sexual relations of moral substance whenever they deepen human intimacy and love. . . . Some marriages may make room for additional sexual partners" (Ellison 1994, 239). Even major figures in the field criticize strict adherence to the older rules of sexual fidelity in marriage and are open to the possibility that spouses might rightly have sex with people outside the marriage (Nelson 1979 and 1992 and Ruether and Bianchi 1976). James Nelson, for example, writes that "Personal growth for either wife or husband may well require intimate friendships beside that with the partner. . . . The important thing is interpersonal intimacy, but intercourse cannot be arbitrarily excluded" (1979, 146). According to Nelson, these extramarital sexual relationships can even be good for marriages. Indeed, Nelson suggests that "the participation of a third party might well be an expression of the couple's profound marital fidelity. It all depends" (1992, 152).

Likewise, many books in pastoral care shy away from judgment about divorce. Many ignore the moral decisions and instead focus on how to care for the feelings of divorcing individuals, overlooking the possibility of reevaluating the decision to divorce. Indeed, the books that challenge divorce most forcefully are not explicitly religious at all (Weiner-Davis 1992, Whitehead 1997, Gallagher 1996, and Schlessinger 1995 and 1996).

Of course, there are reasons behind the turn to self-fulfillment and the hesitation to remind parishioners of obligation and sacrifice. It is, in part, a compensation for the excesses and abuses of the obligation model. If love as self-fulfillment is on one side of the continuum, love as self-loss and negation are on the other. One problem with the obligation model is that it can be abused to pressure people who are weak to sacrifice themselves for the sake of the strong and powerful. Some defenders of the obligation model call for sacrifice and suffering even in the face of repeated transgressions and unfaithfulness of the other. This can be an excuse for sadistic abuse and control on one side and passive masochism on the other. For example, in Margie's case, her insistence on her obligation to sacrifice as an obedient wife serves to excuse her passivity and her failure to protect her children and also allows her husband to continue the abuse without accountability. Neither the extreme self-fulfillment model nor the sacrifice model provides the best resource for moral guidance.

This is the terrain in which Christians live. How can guides find a faithful path between the different models of marriage, promoting the good changes and challenging the bad? How can pastoral care become an instrument of healing in American families?

Moral Guides as Tightrope Walkers: The Pastoral Response

The stress on the extremes of self-fulfillment and self-sacrifice reflects a deep problem in contemporary models of marriage and love. The two distorted options in contemporary life—the model of fulfillment as self-interest and personal satisfaction and the model of obligation as one-sided sacrifice "no matter what" are the worst sides of the goal and rule ethics outlined above. The self-fulfillment model ignores two Christian convictions—that one is called to fulfill responsibilities, often at a cost to oneself, and that one finds ultimate fulfillment by serving God and fulfilling one's (often costly) responsibilities. But in the Christian tradition at its best, the model of sacrificial obligation also has limits. One sacrifices for the sake of others with whom one is in covenant. But in some cases, when the covenant is broken by one side, the other may be justified to change the terms. In marriage, for example, when adultery or abandonment breaks the covenant, the wronged party may redefine the faithful response. Faithful commitment does not always demand self-negation or passive suffering for the sake of another who is not committed to the relationship or who does violence to the partner.

Though these two positions are dangerous in their extreme forms, at their best they offer important lessons for the ministry of pastoral care. The self-fulfillment model reminds caregivers that the growth and immediate happiness of the individual are valuable—within the context of enduring responsibilities. The sacrificial obligation model reminds us of the prior obligation to fulfill costly responsibilities to others, but does not require self-negation for the sake of someone who has breached the covenant and done us violence.

As pastors guide, they can remember that both models make up the moral landscape. Pastors can tailor their responses to the problems of the terrain and the needs of the pilgrims. Gregory Nazianzen used the image of a tightrope walker to describe the balancing act required in pastoral care. Pastors must discern the imbalance before finding the fitting response. If, for example, persons like Margie have little sense of self and submit passively to the brutality of others, then pastoral caregivers may need to guide them toward recognizing their needs and their capacities to take responsibility. But the denial of self is not the only problem. A larger problem in dominant culture is the overemphasis on self-fulfillment to the neglect of responsibilities. How can guides walk the moral tightrope without leaning toward the excesses of self-fulfillment or self-sacrifice?

CHRISTIAN VIEWS OF MARRIAGE, DIVORCE, AND MARITAL SEXUALITY: COMMON AFFIRMATIONS

A pure self-fulfillment model stands in stark contrast to many Christian assumptions about marriage. What resources can moral guides find in the tradition to help them meet the practical needs of parish and culture? Although moral guides find in our tradition a broad consensus on marriage and sexuality, it isn't as simple as consulting a rule book. There are obstacles facing anyone who tries to use all the different rules and principles from Scripture and traditions. One problem is that some rules are outdated. For example, those guilty of adultery are to be put to death (Lev. 20:10) and a man must offer to marry his brother's widow (Deut. 25:5-10). Few Christians today accept these rules or the household codes of the New Testament calling for the obedience of slaves (Titus 2:9 and Eph. 6:5) and regulating women's dress, demeanor, and hairstyle (1 Tim. 2:8-15).

In addition, throughout our tradition, injunctions sometimes contradict each other. Polygamy has been both allowed and prohibited. The rules about divorce also vary widely. And while some parts of Scripture and tradition celebrate the joys of marriage and sex as gifts of God for human life, others (particularly in the New Testament) are more ambivalent about marriage and sexuality (1 Corinthians 7). Followers of Christ were called to leave their families. Celibacy was praised as a higher way (1 Corinthains 7). Some minority voices in our tradition even claimed that sexuality and body were evil. Though the mainstream of Christianity quickly rejected these highly negative viewpoints, our tradition never fully overcame its ambivalence.

The stories of biblical heroes offer questionable models of marriage and sexuality. David messes around with a married woman and then has her husband killed. Abraham's and Sarah's dismissal of Hagar is hardly a model of justice. If these people were nominated for appointment to high positions in the U.S. government, they would never survive confirmation hearings. Our tradition offers a mixed and messy legacy.

But even with these tensions, we find a broad consensus on many points. Some specific rules have been widely accepted. Adultery is proscribed. Rape is prohibited. The faithful are admonished to care for their children, other family members, and the vulnerable of society. There are also broader theological themes regarding sex and marriage. We find celebrations of the goodness of marriage and sex. And we see repeated calls to responsibility in the care of one's family and the fulfillment of one's social obligations. Indeed, two central themes concerning marriage and sexuality are covenant and responsibility. By entering into the marriage covenant, one incurs enduring social obligations and responsibilities.

So, for all the disagreement, there is a broad consensus. And even the criticisms of this consensus don't usually deny primary rules or principles themselves, but instead push the edges of the rules to include new situations and exceptions. We turn to two questions. First, what have been the most widely held rules about marriage in our tradition? Second, how have the rules been extended or modified? (The rules are marked by • and the modifications by *.)

The Form of Marriage

• The major part of Christian tradition has affirmed that marriage is a lifelong covenant, instituted by God, between two people.

* Many Christians have insisted that even though the covenant should be for life, it can be dissolved in extreme cases. A tiny minority of Christians have approved of polygamy. Luther, for example, claimed that bigamy was allowable in extraordinary cases to avoid a greater wrong—like divorce or abandonment. Also, though the vast majority of our tradition has limited this covenant to one man and one woman, some contemporary Christians believe that a covenant may be established between two men or two women.

The Purposes of Marriage

• Within Christian traditions, the marriage covenant, a good gift of God, has many purposes. The covenant is intended primarily for the procreation and care of children as well as for companionship, care, security, growth in faith and character, spiritual communion, and sexual satisfaction. Marriage also forms the core of the family, which, in some parts of our tradition, is the central organizing unit and the hub for religious practice, work, and care for extended family and other vulnerable people.

* Some recent Christians have included as purposes of marriage an array of therapeutic goals—self-fulfillment, inner growth, the healing of childhood wounds, and individuation. These additions can be seen as extensions of the ancient purposes of mutual benefit and growth in character. As long as these additions are subordinate to the other guidelines for marital commitment, they are not negations of the consensus but merely extensions. But if the focus on self-fulfillment becomes the overriding value, trumping or negating other claims, then the traditional model is not simply revised; it is overturned. In Linda's case, for example, her extreme focus on self-fulfillment to the exclusion of any recognition of her obligations flies in the face of the demands of Christian discipleship.

The Obligations of Marriage

• The marriage covenant produces enduring obligations. Each partner is sexually faithful and provides care for the other and the family unit. Normally, these obligations and responsibilities remain even if other purposes of marriage (mutual benefit or procreation) go unfulfilled. Thus, the covenant is both mutual and one-sided.

* Many Christians believe that these enduring obligations can sometimes be dissolved in extreme circumstances when the other has failed in a grave way. For Karen and Margie in the stories above, are the circumstances extreme enough to break those enduring obligations? In Margie's case, does her obligation to her children necessitate that she separate from her husband?

The Dissolution of Marriage

• Christian traditions have a strong presumption against divorce. It is permissible, if at all, only in exceptional circumstances—the most common being adultery.

* Some Christians have added abuse, severe addictions, and even extreme incompatibility as grounds for divorce. Some earlier Christians also included abandonment and sexual dysfunction on the list. (Luther suggested, however, that in cases of sexual dysfunction, bigamy was preferable to divorce or abandonment.) Some Orthodox Christians permit divorce on the grounds of "prolonged imprisonment," "incurable madness," life-threatening domestic violence, apostasy, or even "implacable hatred" (Ware 1995, 531). In Margie's case, many Christians would see clear grounds for divorce.

* Some recent Christians have focused on mutual self-fulfillment as a necessary component of the marriage covenant. Marriages that lack fulfillment may be dissolved. In extreme forms, this change is not so much an addition to traditional models as it is an outright reversal.

Sexual Intercourse

• According to the broad consensus of Christian tradition, sexual intercourse is permissible only within marriage. Adultery is strictly forbidden.

* Some Christians suggest that single adults who are engaged may have sexual intercourse. Luther refused to condemn intercourse for engaged couples, because they had already established a lifelong commitment.

* Some recent statements insist that sexual relationships, whether in marriage or dating, should be just, loving, and consensual. Thus, sex within marriage can be immoral if it lacks these characteristics. And, according to some contemporary Christians, sex outside of marriage can be moral if it has these characteristics. From this perspective, Linda's adultery would not necessarily be wrong. With a few recent exceptions, however, the Christian rejection of adultery and casual sex has remained steadfast. (Christian practice is another matter.)

Sexuality

• Much of the Christian tradition affirms that sexuality is both a good gift of God and has potential for sin and misuse.

* One strand of our tradition is less confident about the goodness of sexuality and focuses more closely on its potential sin and on its subordination to the higher state of celibacy.

* Though the dominant strand of Christian tradition has emphasized the goodness of marital sexuality, some recent Christians have pushed the affirmation further, affirming sexuality while dramatically de-emphasizing sexuality's dangers and its potential for sin.

Walking the Tightrope: Reflecting on the Challenges

Five points from this brief overview are significant to our discussion. First, we find substantial agreement in this broad consensus of Christian tradition—particularly on many issues that are most common to the parish. Second, most of the disagreements concern forms and exceptions. Crudely put, the controversies are about "Who can do what to whom and under what circumstances?" Third, these disagreements about forms and exceptions have not undermined the larger, constant claims about enduring obligations and responsibilities of marriage partners—until recently.

Fourth, we are now witnessing a dramatic transformation. Recent shifts in American culture and Christian pastoral theology make self-fulfillment a primary norm for marriage trumping other norms and even undercutting enduring obligations. Fifth, this transformation includes much higher expectations of marriage than ever before. People not only value self-fulfillment, but actually expect to find it in marriage. The rising divorce rates suggest that these high expectations are not being met.

At the heart of this transformation is a deep shift in ideas. We have a new model of marriage where placing one's own fulfillment above one's obligations to others is not only permissible, but even virtuous. This revolution of ideas and practice confronts pastoral caregivers with serious challenges. They are called on to tend the wounded. Just as important, they are guides in the shift of ideas. This shift challenges fundamental Christian convictions. The overriding focus on individual self-fulfillment, to the neglect of enduring responsibilities, challenges Christian models not only of marriage, but also of faithful discipleship. If life is ultimately about immediate self-fulfillment, then our deepest convictions about discipleship are made void. This is no small shift in moral theology; it is the overturning of Christian faith.

Here's the tricky part: The transformation hasn't been all bad. It's important not to overlook the benefits of the marriage revolution. In our time, we have seen greater equality between men and women than ever before. More fathers are active caregivers of children. More mothers have the chance to pursue education and employment outside the home. Growing wages and economic opportunities for women ease poverty and make the tasks of single motherhood a little easier. This economic independence, along with legal changes, makes it easier for women to protect themselves and their children from abuse. Growing expectations of marriage as a place of fulfillment have prompted many couples to improve their marriages. The divorced and single are not as stigmatized as they were previously. Thus, the shifts bring both problems and benefits.

Given these problems and possibilities, what can pastors do—to guide not only actions but also ideas? Pastors and other Christian caregivers can talk about the weaknesses of the self-fulfillment model and its destructive consequences. They can form Christian communities that train people to be faithful to responsibilities while watching for the excesses of the obligation model. They can do these and other things, but unless pastors dig to the roots of this shift—to the theological problems and human sickness that lie beneath it—their responses will always be inadequate.

WHAT'S OUR PROBLEM?: REMEMBERING A THEOLOGY OF THE ORDINARY

Given these challenges, what should pastors do? The tightrope walker and physician metaphors illumine the pastor's task. Solving a problem demands two steps familiar to a good physician—diagnosing the sickness and finding the best remedy. Or, like Gregory Nazianzen's tightrope walker, the person senses imbalances and then compensates, always being careful not to lean too far in one direction. The moral guide as tightrope walker asks, "How are we imbalanced and what can we do to compensate?" The moral guide as physician asks, "What is the sickness and fitting prescription?" In old-fashioned terms, what is the sin for which we seek a remedy?

One common way to make sense of our current problem goes like this. People fail in their responsibilities because they don't value something enough. So, the remedy is to encourage them to value it. If children are irresponsible with money, for example, good parents will talk with them about its value. Following this same line of thinking, someone could arrive at one possible explanation for our rampant failure of responsibility. Perhaps we fail to be responsible because we don't value marriage and sexuality highly enough. In fact, this seems to be the dominant mindset among many religious people today. Many mainline voices have responded to the crisis of responsibility by reminding people of the value of marriage, sexuality, and body. Whether in theology, pastoral care, ethics, or preaching, many Christian leaders trumpet the joys of sexuality and of intimacy in marriage. They also offer concrete practical advice on making them better. They develop theologies around the goodness and sanctity of bodies, sexuality, and other aspects of creation.[4] These things are valued in themselves and as primary avenues of human fulfillment and divine presence. Many Protestants, Catholics, New Agers, liberals, and evangelicals have moved to sanctify the ordinary. Even the current revival of interest in spirituality is not about "otherworldliness" but this-worldliness. It is a spirituality of the commonplace. At one level, this move is a powerful renewal of key biblical themes, a reminder of the importance of creation and incarnation. It is an occasion to praise God.

This remedy (sanctifying the ordinary) relies on a particular diagnosis (the failure to value the ordinary). There is one snag. What if the remedy is based on a false diagnosis? What if the prescription does not fit our core sickness? Is our core problem that we don't value the world highly enough? What if the problem of dominant culture is not that we undervalue things, but that we overvalue them—or value them in the wrong way?

I believe that we are irresponsible about marriage and sexuality not because we think too little of them, but because we expect too much. In old-fashioned language, the overriding sin of our age is idolatry. We attempt to find ultimate fulfillment in the ordinary.

This culture and its inhabitants (including Linda and Karen) expect more of marriage and sexuality than any generation before it. We expect perfect mates, perfect bodies, perfect orgasms, perfect children, perfect moods, and perfect families. Because approximately 100 percent of us grow up in imperfect families, we then expect to find perfect healing of those childhood wounds in perfect families of adulthood. And because most of us came with less-than-perfect bodies that would, if left to their own devices, sink and sag lower by the minute, we work to perfect them—with barbells and stair-steppers, tummy tucks and face-lifts. Our expectations don't stop with the relationships of our households or the functions of our bodies. We also expect perfect politicians, perfect churches, perfect jobs, perfect ecosystems, and the perfect cup of coffee. And we expect it all on easy terms, satisfaction guaranteed or your money back. When, inevitably, we don't find these perfect mates, families, and communities, we feel dissatisfied and even cheated. We may leave our imperfect relationships in search of perfect mates and communities. Or we may even give up the search and flee from commitment altogether. On the other side, we may value that other person too much, completely negating ourselves and giving over our identities and wills.

Is it any accident that the culture with the highest expectations for marriage has produced the highest rates of divorce, the lowest rates of marriage, and a growing number of people afraid to make any commitments at all? Our failures of responsibility stem not from undervaluing things but overvaluing them. We expect not too little but too much.

If the sin is expecting too much of the ordinary, then the remedy isn't simply to remind people of the extraordinary nature of the ordinary. Remember the tightrope walker. If the problem is that we overvalue the ordinary, then praising it to the heavens will simply throw us further off balance. The fitting response is not just a reminder of the sanctity of the ordinary, but a renewed sense of the ordinariness of the ordinary. The remedy is a new realism about the ordinary. To combat the problem of irresponsibility, we need not a higher, but a lower view of marriage and sexuality.

This new realism has several components. First, a new realism insists that human relationships of marriage and sex are ordinary parts of creation that are always imperfect and fragile. They are good on one day, mediocre the next, and a pain in the backside on more days than we care to admit. If we expect perfection and ultimate fulfillment in these relationships, we will be disappointed. Having realistic expectations allows us to accept relationships and persons for what they are—always imperfect and often wonderful. Second, the new realism reminds us that any human activity or relationship is subject to sin and distortion. With greater awareness we can build in structures for protection and accountability.[5] Third, the ordinary, however good and sacred, can never be ultimately fulfilling. Only God provides ultimate fulfillment. Precisely because things are not right with us, we need a Savior. We remember not only creation and incarnation, but also sin and redemption. We need a new realism about marriage.

But that isn't the whole story, either. No matter how great the imbalance, tightrope walkers must take care not to overcompensate, sending us off-balance in another direction. We need more than a new realism. We need a new idealism that sets marriage in proper perspective, helping us to see it for what it is, an extraordinary gift of God and a calling with a divine purpose. Yes, marriage is subject to all the limits of finite creation. It is, at the same time, wonderfully human, sometimes miraculous, and always embraced in the arms of grace and infused with divine purpose. We cannot forget either the ordinariness or the sanctity of the ordinary.

A hopeful realism and a chastened idealism can help Christian tightrope walkers remember both sides, never leaning too far, learning how to adjust according to the imbalance of the era and the needs of parishioners. Only by discerning these different needs, says Gregory Nazianzen, can pastors guide "according to the methods of a pastoral care which is right and just, and worthy of our true Shepherd" (1995, II.34, 212).

WHAT THEN SHALL WE DO? : A RETURN TO THE CASES

How do we apply these reflections to our three cases? Linda, Karen, and Margie expect too much of marriage, though in very different ways. Linda is leaving her family for a lover because she had expected her marriage to yield greater self-fulfillment and happiness than any normal relationship could. It is even less likely that the new relationship will bring that fulfillment. In addition, Linda values the marriage covenant too little and breaks it too easily. Karen is also pulled by high expectations of marriage found in popular culture. These expectations make it even harder to deal with the struggles around her husband's anxiety. Even Margie expects too much. She expects Jack to be something he isn't. She values him too highly, giving over her self, her self-worth, and her responsibility to her children in deference to him. This is idolatry. What do Pastors Johnson, Olsen, and Miles think about the situations they face? More important, how should they respond?

Tom Johnson was troubled by Linda Wilson's adultery and her decision to leave her family. He shares the consensus of the Christian tradition that adultery is wrong and also believes that marriage vows should be honored except in extraordinary circumstances. He worries that Linda has unrealistic expectations of marriage and is making decisions based on her own immediate happiness while forgetting her responsibilities to others. He wonders if she could come to see her situation differently or at least slow down the process of divorce? Tom recognizes that

Linda won't easily see these problems because she is blinded by the new love of an adulterous relationship. He considers referral, but because the marriage counselors in his area work out of a self-fulfillment model, he worries that referral would be the fastest route to divorce.

Later in the week, Linda stops by the office to apologize for blowing up at Tom, adding "I just have so much going on inside. I'm confused." He invites her into the office. After listening to Linda describe her feelings of frustration and offering sympathetic responses, he acknowledges her feelings and then shifts the focus.

> It's no wonder you're feeling confused. You are feeling many different pulls—your love for your daughters, your tie to David, your attraction to Peter, your conscience, and your responsibilities. I want to ask a few questions to give us a clearer sense of the factors and options. You can answer now or think about them later.

Tom poses a series of questions about the people involved, the options she faces, the consequences of each option, etc. He begins by getting basic information and looking for missing or overlooked factors. Has there been abuse in the marriage? If so, are the daughters in danger of abuse? Has Peter agreed to a definite plan to marry her soon after their divorce? (Often the lover is not interested in a long-term relationship but never actually says it.) How are the daughters handling the stress? (She may have forgotten to pay attention to them. This can recall her to responsibility.) Tom also begins talking through options. Notice that he asks questions and provides options in a direct, leading way. He also emphasizes her capacity to choose and to be responsible.

> Let's lay out all the possible options and decisions. The first decision is whether or not to divorce. You don't have make that decision now. [Delay is one of the few effective tactics with someone "in love." It gives time for a return to sanity.] The second decision you face is how you will choose to respond to the adultery. Let's look at all the possible options. What are all the options you see? . . . Okay, you've named the two polar opposites— moving in with Peter immediately or quitting the affair immediately and continuing in the same old patterns with David. Can you think of other options?

Linda sarcastically replies, "I suppose I could always become a nun or escape to the rain forest." Tom responds, "Hmm. Linda in the convent or the jungle. I'm not sure which seems the most unlikely. Have you considered the French Foreign Legion?" They both laugh and begin spinning out unlikely scenarios. Tom continues:

In addition to convent, jungle, and pirate ship, some women in your situation have tried other, less creative options—initiating a waiting period where they are not involved with either man but have a chance to think things through or initiating a waiting period where they remain at home but have a contract with their husband limiting the interactions. Can you think of others?

Another step is to ask Linda about the consequences of the various options before her. Tom could say:

Now that we have the options and decisions before us, let's think about the consequences for different people. I've seen you with your daughters and know how much they mean to you. Let's start with them. What effect might the different options have on them? [Tom could also ask about other people.]

A next step is to give Linda some things to think about before the next session. If pushed to choose now, she will probably leave her family. So he's planting seeds and trying to delay decisions. Tom could ask Linda to consider a few exercises from the list in chapter 2. "I have an exercise in creativity for you to think about over the next week. Imagine you are at the end of your life and are engaged in a life review. When you come to this time, what decisions and actions would you feel proudest about?"

Another step is to offer sobering stories and statistics for Linda to think about after the session. Tom could give an honest accounting of some of the difficulties that people in Linda's situation face without insisting that they apply to Linda. This provides a generous dose of realism.

I want to tell some stories about people in similar situations, even though I don't know that your experience would be like theirs. Many years ago a woman came to me in a similar situation. She moved away from her husband and children to be with another man. They were deeply in love and she planned for them to establish a home together for her children. Six months after the divorce, they broke up. Her husband did not want to remarry her, but he retained custody of their children. Of course, not all affairs end like this. But as you mull over your decisions, you need to know that most do. Seventy-five percent of extramarital affairs end soon after they become public. Around 8 or 9 percent of people having affairs marry. And that small group has a high divorce rate. That means that, at the highest, only 3 to 4 percent of people having affairs end up in long-term marriages with their lover. Almost 100 percent of the people I counsel believe that they are in that 3 percent. And maybe you would be in that 3 percent. I don't know. But in addition to thinking about the moral questions, as you consider the future, you might keep in mind these facts from the experiences of other people. [Pause for Linda to comment.]

The other question to consider is the effect on your daughters. When I worked mostly with youth, I spent many hours with teenagers whose parents were divorcing. They not only grieved about the divorce, but were affected in other ways. Their grades dropped and they began to get into trouble. Many still have a rough time—trouble with jobs, marriages, addictions, mental illness, and the law. Perhaps your daughters' stories would be nothing like theirs. But a primary factor you need to consider is the potential effect on your daughters. Children of divorce have two to five times the rates of psychological problems, school suspensions, unemployment, and divorce. Here's a one-page summary of statistics. I can't know what you or your daughters would experience, but I do know that you need to have all the facts.

Giving parents the facts and statistics is not cruel. Many well-meaning parents decide to divorce because they believe that children are not harmed. That is a myth. Long-term studies suggest that only in cases of extreme conflict are children helped by a divorce. Knowing the truth is crucial to making a responsible decision. So, moral guides have a responsibility to tell parishioners the truth.

As hinted above, delay is an effective strategy when people are in romantic affairs. Because they are so blind, holding off a decision until their vision improves may be the best option. Tom could say:

I want you to consider taking some time with these decisions. Right now you feel under tremendous pressure. But there is no hurry. If you and Peter are in that 3 percent, a little time will not break the bond. By taking the time, you'll be able to work with your daughters and David. You don't have to answer now. Just think about it.

At some point, perhaps in a later conversation, Tom will need to tell Linda directly what he thinks about her actions and what the church says about committing adultery and leaving one's family. Knowing that they will be in long-term conversation, he is trying to walk a narrow line and avoid outright confrontation. When he decides the time is right, he could say something like this:

When you decided to come see me, your pastor, you probably didn't expect that I would approve of adultery. So, you won't be surprised by what I'm going to say. In our church, we believe that sex belongs in marriage and that people have responsibilities that are more important than finding immediate fulfillment. If you choose to continue in the adultery and to leave your family, you will be turning your back on sacred responsibilities. Your decisions could have devastating consequences for others, especially for your daughters. In our tradition, we believe that God expects more of us.

Also, Tom may eventually initiate a very direct conversation about the liabilities of different models of marriage. He could address the weakness of the self-fulfillment model more directly. He could introduce a conversation about the life of Christian faithfulness and discipleship.

Like Tom Johnson and the broad Christian consensus, Pastor Judy Olsen values the lifelong covenant of marriage. She also believes that divorce is morally acceptable in exceptional circumstances such as adultery, abuse, severe addictions, and abandonment. When children are being abused, Judy believes that divorce or separation is not only permitted but even recommended.

Judy also knows that Margie objects to all divorce and believes that wives should be obedient and long-suffering. She also suspects that Margie does not value herself. She wonders how Margie might come to feel that she is a beloved child of God. She wonders how to challenge Margie's notion of the extreme self-sacrifice and suffering. How might Margie come to see that she is not just a passive victim, but is responsible for making choices that are good for herself and her children? Whether Margie stays or leaves the marriage, the children's future depends on Margie taking responsibility. Judy also knows that Margie's options are limited. She has four young children, no previous job experience, and fifty-five dollars in the bank. How can Judy take these realities into account when counseling with Margie?

When Margie comes for counseling, Judy decides to guide the conversation in two directions—to help Margie explore her responsibilities to her children and to recognize her own strength and worth. Judy begins with the first, because she hopes that Margie's natural strength will emerge as she thinks about protecting her children. Eventually, she also wants to guide Margie into a discussion of marriage that might help her to rethink her understanding of submission and even to consider leaving her husband. Before she introduces these topics, though, she listens to Margie and asks questions about what is happening now in the family. She also "brush clears," steering Margie away from side issues. Judy introduces the question about responsibility to the children by asking crucial questions.

> Watching you with your kids, I see how much you love them. I remember several years ago—when Jack hit Christina—how hard that was on you. In addition to that one time, have you ever seen any signs or even suspected at any time that Jack was abusing them? . . . Have you watched to make sure? . . . Have you ever asked the children if they have been abused? . . . Would you ask them and watch them to be sure?

These questions are important not only to remind Margie to take responsibility for her children. In addition, if Judy finds reason to suspect child abuse, she must notify the authorities immediately. After this conversation, Judy can remind Margie of both her responsibility to her children and her forgotten strength. Judy might say:

> Our Scriptures teach us that caring for children is a sacred responsibility. I've seen you shoulder that responsibility for your children. When it comes to protecting your babies, you can sometimes be as strong as a mother bear. Now, if you decide to stay with Jack, your first responsibility as a mother is to protect your children. That responsibility is more important than being an obedient wife or pleasing Jack. It's more important than anything else.

Judy can then place questions before Margie in an almost liturgical form. "Will you be strong for your kids? . . . Will you protect them from all abuse? . . . Will you find ways to renew your strength? . . . Will you give your daughters a good model for being a strong woman? . . . Will you teach and show your sons that it is wrong to abuse women and children?" Another step is to talk with Margie about ways that she can find strength. Using the techniques outlined in chapter 2, Judy could help Margie identify the exceptional times in the past when she did find strength and turn to activities or things that remind her of that strength.

Judy also wants to remind Margie of her own value. One of the best strategies is simply to state it as a conviction of faith, almost in confessional form. Judy begins with the value of the kids, which Margie sees, and then moves to Margie's value. This could be an appropriate closing to their conversation. Judy could say confidently:

> Margie, I believe that you can do what you have to protect yourself and your kids. They are good kids and worth protecting. But that's not all. You are worth protecting. You are a valuable and beloved child of God. God looks at you and rejoices. Do you hear me, Margie? I know how much you love your kids. God's love for you and your children is even greater than that. Do you know that?

After closing in prayer, Judy schedules an appointment with Margie for the next week. They plan to talk about how things are going. Judy also wants to ask Margie again if she has seen any abuse. If child abuse is suspected, Judy will not only report the abuse, but also be much more direct about Margie's responsibility to take immediate steps to protect the children. At some point, perhaps in the next conversation, Judy plans to talk with Margie about her understanding of divorce, male headship, and female submission. Her primary concern is to help Margie see some of the distortions of extreme models of sacrificial love and submissive obedience.

Finally, what did I think and do about Karen and Larry? I wasn't convinced that Larry's problems justified divorce. Just as important, I suspected that Karen doubted it, too. I also recognized that Karen was toying with questionable ideas about marriage—that it is supposed to meet all her needs. This model stands in contrast to dominant Christian assumptions about marriage. It is also highly unrealistic. I was cautious about this perspective, and, after several conversations, I sensed that Karen was, too. Consequently, I directed the conversation into a discussion of models of marriage and the problems with the self-fulfillment model. I also suspected that this wasn't the only issue. Karen was strongly pulled by the obligation and self-sacrifice model. Perhaps some of her unhappiness in the marriage came from trying, unsuccessfully, to meet all of Larry's needs and submerging her own. So, I also decided to guide us into a conversation about her own fulfillment and needs, but in the context of marital commitment.

So what did I do? First, I asked her to describe what was going on. And I asked leading questions to find any significant overlooked factors. "Has there been any abuse? Are you or Larry in an adulterous relationship? Are you in love with or attracted to someone else?" (Often the question of divorce emerges when one partner is strongly attracted to another person.)

I also asked about options and consequences. "What options do you see?" At first Karen saw only two options—divorce or keeping things the way they were. So I added, "There might be some 'in-between' options, like postponing the question of divorce and experimenting with the marriage. Because we share a commitment to marriage, it might make sense to put the divorce question to the side for a while and consider some 'in-between' steps."

There are many different ways that Karen might experiment with the marriage. She could examine times when things were better in their marriage, asking what she did differently. Perhaps she was busy with her job and friends and had less time to ruminate about the marriage or to push Larry for greater intimacy. With less pressure, Larry may have felt freer to be in relationship. I asked Karen to think about exceptional times, to discern what she was doing differently, and to try to repeat those differences.

One approach to use in Karen's case is to "assume the best" and speak it. I said something like this, "Karen, one of the reasons that I want you to consider these experiments and to delay divorce is that I sense you are very hesitant about divorce. If you were certain, you would be having appointments with lawyers not counselors. I have a feeling that you share our tradition's strong presumption against divorce. Frankly, I'm glad." The conversation can then shift to a conversation about models of marriage. "All of us confront many different ways of looking at marriage. I want you to think about your model of marriage. What is marriage? How does your model compare to the models around you? Most important, what difference does your Christian faith make for the way you see marriage?" This conversation will usually require lots of direction. People aren't used to thinking about theology and the purpose of marriage. The pastor can talk openly about the weaknesses of the models. The purpose of this conversation with Karen is to address the difficulties of expecting ultimate fulfillment in marriage or becoming resigned to self-sacrifice and ignoring her needs. The pastor can even directly challenge parishioners' models.

When human needs and fulfillment are seen as one part of a larger responsible life, pastors can introduce practical suggestions about getting needs met. One exercise I suggested for Karen was to think about seeking other avenues for fulfillment while remaining married to Larry.

> I want you to make a list of some of your primary needs. Can you list some of them now? . . . Good. No one human relationship can or should meet all our needs. Indeed, the primary task of Christian life is not to have our needs met. But they are still important. How can some of these needs be responsibly met in other places? Could you list a few specific ways that some of the other needs can be met? . . . Good. In the next week, try two of these steps. Then look for other ways that your needs could be met by people outside the marriage. Maybe you and a friend could talk every afternoon about work frustrations. Maybe you and your brother could go dancing. In the end, these steps may not only be good for you but also for Larry. The best way to care for him may be to give him some room.

The primary purpose of these exercises was to refocus Karen's attention. The ultimate goal was not to find immediate self-fulfillment "no matter what," but to find fulfillment within the context of her obligations and also to let off some of the intense pressure so that they could begin to establish as strong a marriage as possible.

STEPS FOR PRACTICAL APPLICATION IN THE PARISH

Though these stories are fairly common in pastoral counseling, a good pastor must be ready to respond to a larger variety of cases. Moreover, good pastors prepare themselves and parishioners to live faithfully and think through the issues before crises begin. What practical steps can churches and pastors take?

Theology of Marriage and Sexuality:
Teaching, Preaching, and Transforming

Know your Christian theology of marriage. Preach and teach about it. Also help parishioners to articulate their Christian theology of marriage.

Ask questions of your model and the models of parishioners. How does your model compare to other Christian models and current practices in the culture? How is your model challenged by others?

Name the demons. Honor the possibilities. In teaching, preaching, and counseling, talk openly about the challenges, dangers, and opportunities facing marriages today.

Take authority. In pulpit and counseling office, interpret the issues from the standpoint of faith and through the lens of Christian theology.

Read about patterns of marriage and divorce in American culture. By looking at the statistics and patterns, you will find new insights about human lives. Recommend readings to others. (See bibliography.)

Learn about changes in marriage and divorce laws. Many states are considering initiatives to make divorces harder to obtain unless both sides consent, to give extra protection to the needs of children and homemakers, and to enact mandatory counseling and longer waiting periods for couples applying for marriage licenses. Work to support changes that give preference to the needs of children and to slow divorce rates, while providing quick help for victims of domestic violence.

In counseling session and classroom, be a realist and idealist about marriage. Remind yourself and parishioners that marriage is both a joy and a pain. Remind the romanticists of its messiness. Remind the cynics of its holy purposes. Find the balance of a tightrope walker.

Pastoral Counseling

Become a divorce buster. Make a commitment to marriage. Unless the marriage in question is rent by severe problems (abuse or abandonment), work with the couple or individual to salvage the marriage. If children are involved, redouble your efforts. Therapists and pastors whose clients have low divorce rates share one thing in common—a partiality to the marriage covenant.

Make a commitment to learn techniques that help marriages survive. Read Michele Weiner-Davis's *Divorce Busting* and recommend similar books to couples and other counselors.

Remember that pastoral care is a ministry not only of presence but also of guidance. By providing direction in counseling, guides help pilgrims find a faithful path.

Know how to recognize exceptional cases. Know the signs of abuse. If a partner is being abused, work with her to seek help immediately. If the abuse is recurring, talk seriously about separation and divorce. If the couple has children, discuss the terrible effects of spouse abuse on children. If children are abused, contact the appropriate social services agency immediately and redouble your efforts to get nonabusing spouses to take responsibility for the safety of their children and themselves.

Prepare for abuse cases by talking about the problem in pulpit and classroom, visiting agencies that work with survivors, and reading basic information. Get materials from women's shelters and county mental-health facilities. Keep extra pamphlets on domestic violence in your office, on church bulletin boards, and in restrooms.

Prepare yourself and parishioners long before couples come for counseling. Read about sex and marriage in U.S. culture, know your theology of marriage, and learn pastoral care strategies to help marriages. Prepare parishioners by naming these problems from the pulpit and helping them build stronger marriages.

In marital and premarital counseling, take a marriage history. What are the models of marriage they have known? What issues and problems most commonly arose? Given that history, what do they want to avoid? What do they want to find? What are the models of marriage of exemplary couples they know?

Remember the universal rule of difference. The best counseling approach will vary according to differences in personality, sins, and virtues. The pastor is always a tightrope walker seeking the right balance.

Give greater attention to premarital counseling. Require more sessions. Find training resources for yourself and reading materials for couples. Find a good questionnaire that can reveal areas of potential conflict.

Ask couples to sign Christian "prenuptial commitments." While most prenuptial agreements make it easier to leave a marriage, Christian prenuptial commitments make it harder. Ask them to write and sign an agreement committing themselves to a waiting period and a process of mediation if they later confront problems. The couple could choose close friends to "witness" the signing and to remind them of its terms in the event of later problems.

Work closely with engaged couples, particularly adult children of divorce, to identify good, long-lasting marriages among friends, family, and church members. Judith Wallerstein's book *The Good Marriage* is a helpful resource.

Ask engaged parishioners to interview a half dozen couples with good marriages. Ask several couples with strong marriages to volunteer for these interviews. If the engaged couple hits it off with an exemplary couple, ask them to talk further in the first year of marriage.

Find counseling centers that have specialized services for engaged couples. Make sure that their values are compatible with Christian models of marriage.

Emphasize the responsibilities of community. At the wedding rehearsal, give a short talk about the responsibilities of friends and family to support the couple as they build a strong marriage and work through problems.

Give special attention to people marrying again after divorce. Engage them in discussions about the previous marriage and how they can avoid the same mistakes.

Schedule follow-up appointments within the first year of marriage. The most difficult issues often appear after the couple has the security of the marriage relationship.

Talk with engaged couples about the changes common after marriage. Many cohabiting couples and others with long engagements are shocked when the security of marriage allows room for difficult issues to emerge for the first time.

When working with married couples experiencing other crises (death of a child or loss of work) remind them that these problems can be devastating on marriages. Help them devise a plan for nurturing the marriage. Check in with them in the months following the crisis. Connect them with healthy couples who have weathered similar crises.

When parents consider divorce, ask them to consider the consequences for their children. Give them statistics. It is important for them to know all the facts before they decide.

When couples with children decide to divorce, help them devise both a plan for making the divorce easier on children and a procedure for regular consultation about the children's needs. Encourage noncustodial parents to take responsibility for their children.

Work closely with married couples who have children. Offer a summary of statistics about the effects of divorce on children. Form support and discussion groups for couples with children and for single parents.

Develop mentoring programs pairing couples in newer marriages with older couples in solid, committed marriages.

Encourage couples to enroll in good marriage-enrichment programs.

Support single parents. Establish networks for practical tasks like taking children to piano lessons. Find exemplary parishioners who could be mentors and extended family to children of single-parent families. Form support groups.

Work closely with children and teenagers. Teach them about marriage and commitment. Have couples in good marriages talk with youth.

Offer support and counseling to children of divorce. Establish procedures to support children in the divorce transition. The stability of seeing old friends and participating in familiar routines can ease their suffering.

Set up ongoing support groups for divorced members as well as new widows and widowers.

Promote ministries with single people. Don't belittle singleness. How could we demean the state so highly praised in the New Testament and practiced by Jesus?

Be careful about referral, ensuring that counselors share similar values. Do not refer couples to divorce-friendly counselors. Do not refer domestic violence cases to divorce-prohibiting counselors.

Know your limits and God's grace. A popular magazine asks, "Can this marriage be saved?" One thing is certain: A pastor can't save it. A pastor can only guide and trust in God's unfailing grace.

5

KEEPING WATCH OVER THE SHEPHERDS BY DAY AND NIGHT
Sexual Misconduct and Accountability among Moral Guides

Therefore, you shepherds, hear the word of the Lord: "As I live, says the Lord God, because my sheep have become prey, and my sheep have become food for all the wild animals, since there was no shepherd. . . . Thus says the Lord God, I am against the shepherds; and I will demand my sheep at their hand, and put a stop to their feeding the sheep; no longer shall the shepherds feed themselves. I will rescue my sheep from their mouths, so that they may not be food for them.
—Ezekiel 34:7-10

If the shepherd keeps watch over the sheep, who keeps watch over the shepherd? If pastors are moral guides, who guides them? Two of the greatest blots on the church are clergy misconduct and the failure to hold abusive ministers accountable. Though we focus here on sexual misconduct, many of the strategies for accountability and prevention could apply to other issues.[1]

Of all clergy misconduct, sexual misconduct is especially reprehensible.[2] Most pastors know a dozen horror stories. A pastor new to a congregation discovers that the former pastor was a predator, having had sexual intercourse with several counselees. An associate pastor is told by a trusted parishioner that the senior pastor is "having an affair" with a married church member. A boy is molested by his pastor. Troubled by shame and loss of trust, he never tells another soul.

WHEN SHEPHERDS PREY: SURVEYING THE PROBLEM

These are not isolated incidents. The statistics on clergy sexual misconduct are sobering. For every case we see in the newspaper, many others are never reported. Though most victims remain silent, the statistics speak loudly. In the best known study, 12.7 percent of pastors admitted to having had sexual intercourse with a parishioner; 38.6 percent admitted to some "sexual contact." The rate of sexual misconduct is higher for clergy than for other professions, including physicians, social workers, and therapists. More than 75 percent of the clergy report that they know a pastor who has had sexual intercourse with a parishioner. But if the above statistics are even close to the mark, *every* pastor knows pastors who are guilty of sexual misconduct.[3] In spite of the numbers, the church has been even slower to respond than many other professional groups.

No denominations or theological perspectives are immune to misconduct or the failure of accountability. The issue crosses all lines of age, wealth, ethnicity, and even gender. Though the great majority of abusers are men and most victims are women, that is not always so. Men, particularly younger men and boys, are sometimes victims, and women are sometimes perpetrators. Male and female clergy bear equal responsibility for holding themselves and other pastors accountable. Every pastor is called to "keep watch over the shepherds."

The statistics on clergy sexual misconduct become even more troubling when we remember the devastation it brings. Many survivors of sexual misconduct had come to the pastor to seek help in a time of confusion. After the abuse, they often lose the sense of church as a sanctuary or safe place. Some survivors stop going to church at all and hesitate to trust pastors or even God. Most do not report the abuse and experience isolation and shame in secrecy. And many people who do report are not believed or are blamed for the pastor's misconduct. The damage extends beyond survivors to their families, the families of perpetrators, and the whole church. Even when the incident is never told, the church is diminished. If the church is the body of Christ, then any abuse wounds the whole body. Injury to the body is no less dangerous simply because it is kept secret. Indeed, not knowing and not treating the problem only makes it worse.

Given the gravity of the problem, how can pastors hold themselves and their colleagues accountable? The following stories describe what three pastors have done. The first case is the most common scenario of the three. A minister hears a complaint and does nothing. The second and third cases are not average. The ministers in these cases take decisive action and find a decent resolution. These last two cases, while neither average nor perfect, give a realistic picture of how fallible, responsible pastors and churches can respond. The second and third stories point toward better solutions and outline appropriate steps.

THREE STORIES OF SEXUAL MISCONDUCT

Doing Nothing: Ignore a Perpetrator and Hope He Will Go Away

A layperson tells Karl, an associate pastor, that the senior pastor propositioned her during a counseling session. Having heard that he had propositioned others, she wants someone in a position of responsibility to know. Though she would rather not file charges (in the church, civil or criminal courts) unless others would join her, she gives Karl permission to report the incident and let her know if she should talk with someone else or consider filing charges. He decides not to report, because he believes that he has "no proof" and that he would risk his job. Karl hears occasional rumors, but no other direct allegations.

Ten years later, when Karl is the pastor of another church, he hears that a layperson has filed charges against his former senior pastor. As the accusations are made public, other women come forward with complaints spanning fifteen years. The senior pastor denies everything and strikes out at his accusers. Karl wonders if he had acted differently, might some of these women, their families, and the church have been spared the horror of abuse? He asks what he might do now to help prevent misconduct and to hold perpetrators accountable. The do-nothing approach failed. What should he have done? What should he do now?

Unfortunately, the do-nothing response is common. It is not only morally unconscionable, but also goes against the regulations of most states and many denominations. We are right to condemn the do-nothing approach. But when we are honest, most of us know that we are also charged in that condemnation. Until recently, most pastors have done too little, either to investigate charges or to develop policies for accountability. Karl's senior pastor was a sexual predator who repeatedly abused vulnerable people to satisfy his desire for power and control. Even after abusing many people, perpetrators are often never held accountable. Most perpetrators victimize parishioners who are weak and less likely to make public accusations or to be believed if they do. And if charges are made, predators usually deny everything and use any means to silence accusers. Without clear guidelines, it is next to impossible to bring clergy predators to justice. Even with guidelines, it is hard. Fortunately, many churches have changed. Responding to the call of conscience and the fear of lawsuits and multimillion-dollar settlements, many churches are developing better procedures for responding to clergy sexual misconduct.

Dealing Aggressively with a Sexual Predator

Leonard, a senior pastor, is told by a trusted staff member that the associate pastor, Ben, is having sex with a parishioner. Both the associate and
parishioner are married and have young children. The staff member has
also heard from a minister in another city that Ben had been "involved
with" another parishioner in his previous church. Leonard looks over
church and denominational policies on sexual misconduct and then
takes action. He calls the denominational official to talk through the procedures. Though they agree to begin the process, the denominational
official will call an attorney before setting things in motion. When
Leonard asks if there had been previous suspicion of misconduct, the
denominational official admits that Ben was accused in his former
church, but that official charges were never filed because the senior pastor "hushed things up." Leonard calls Ben into his office and asks him
about the charges. At first, Ben appears offended that Leonard could
"suggest such a thing." When Leonard lays out the evidence, Ben admits
to having had a brief "affair." Leonard explains why Ben's actions are
unethical and unprofessional and goes over the procedures for clergy
sexual misconduct.

Leonard then calls the woman to explain the steps he is taking and
why. He tells her that the investigation is solely against the pastor. She
does not want to file charges, but says that she and Ben had sex several
times after she went to him for marriage counseling. Leonard offers to
arrange for her to get counseling at the church's expense and invites her
to talk with him or the church's pastoral counselor. He also tries to begin
a conversation about the fallout of clergy sexual abuse experienced by
many survivors. But for now, she is focused only on her fear that her husband will find out. Leonard promises to call back the next day. Hearing
her distress, he is furious—with Ben for his misconduct, with other pastors for failing to hold Ben accountable, and with himself for not catch-
ing the problem sooner.

Then he gets back to work. He reviews the notes he has made
throughout the day, making sure that he has recorded everything. If the
case should ever come to trial, his notes will be crucial evidence. He tele-
phones the denominational official and the small personnel committee
made up of six leading laypeople, and sets up an emergency meeting that
evening. At the meeting, they agree that if Ben is guilty of repeated misconduct, the risks are too great to have him continue in ministry. The lay
leaders want to offer Ben the option of resigning and surrendering his
clergy credentials. Leonard agrees to their decision. They also decide that
the church will provide funds for counseling for the woman, Ben, and
their families. After trying to talk himself out of trouble, Ben reluctantly
hands over his clergy credentials.

Though the main plot of the story is resolved, the whole church is left with grief and confusion. Leonard addresses the issue in the church newsletter and sermon while trying to be sensitive to the moral and legal demands for confidentiality. Over the next month, Leonard counsels the woman, her family, other members, and staff. Many members are angry. Several don't believe the charges. Others are furious that Ben was sent to their church after previous misconduct. The last Leonard heard, Ben was selling insurance in another state. Because the woman who was abused moved to another church, Leonard can only guess about the long-term effects on her life. He faces another round of unfinished stories. He and his counseling supervisor talk through his frustration.

Both Leonard and Karl faced a sexual predator. Unlike Karl, Leonard used both his power and the procedures to hold Ben accountable and protect others from further abuse. At every step, he followed the procedure, working to protect everyone's rights and to find an acceptable solution. He still wonders if he should have insisted on a church trial. He wishes he could have done more. More important, he asks what he could do now to prevent further misconduct. For all his doubts, Leonard's steps provide one realistic model for dealing responsibly with clergy sexual misconduct.

Wandering: Recognizing the Warning Signs and Responding Appropriately

Newspapers highlight the misconduct of predators, but even more pastors "wander" into misconduct. "Wanderers" engage in sexual misconduct one time at a moment of weakness. They are likely to confess and seek help. While their misconduct is not repeated or as intentionally manipulative as the predators', wanderers can cause just as much damage. Many pastors remember a time when they were at risk for wandering. But if pastors know themselves, watch for danger signs, and set up procedures of accountability, they can avoid wandering. Clergy sexual misconduct is completely preventable. Every pastor must be attentive.

Susan is the pastor of two rural churches, her first appointment out of seminary. Though she gets along well with her parishioners, she is lonely. Their average age is about seventy; that's twice her age. One of the few younger people in the church is Dale, the twenty-one-year-old son of the piano player. Though a lifelong member, he is only at church during breaks from college. Over summer vacation, he and Susan strike up a friendship, meeting twice a week for lunch or coffee. Eventually, he reveals that he was sexually abused as a child. After several conversations about the abuse, Susan recommends that he talk with a local counselor and with the university counselor in the fall. He agrees.

During the fall semester, Dale writes every week. With greater distance, she begins to realize that they had developed a very intimate bond. Remembering several incidents and rereading his letters, she realizes that he has a crush on her. Susan knows that infatuation with a pastor is common. She will simply be careful to keep better boundaries, while not cutting off her friendship to him as his pastor. A few nights later, Susan has an erotic dream about Dale. While she normally doesn't put much stock in dreams, this one makes her recognize that she has been attracted to Dale for a long time. She begins to remember her anticipation before his visits and the intimate things she told him—things that she normally shared only with her closest friends. Though there had been no physical contact, Susan realized that somewhere along the way the boundaries were blurred. For a moment, Susan even fantasized about the possibility of dating Dale. She began to rationalize—they were both adults, and she was not his year-round pastor. But Susan had enough of a conscience to see that no excuse would change the fact that she was his pastor and had even been his counselor. It would never be appropriate for her to act on her attraction to him.

Seeing how oblivious she had been both to his feelings and her own, she felt like a fool. Through conversations with a fellow pastor, she was able to accept the fact of the attraction, while discerning a faithful response. Simply telling about the attraction made it fade. She came up with strategies to reestablish boundaries with Dale in a kind way. More important, she explored the bigger issue—her own needs and how they were not being met. She changed some things, arranging to get supervision with a therapist and to have weekly coffee with other pastors. She also made a pact with a pastor to talk over problems and temptations in ministry.

Many pastors have a story like Susan's. For every pastor who has wandered into misconduct, there are twice as many who narrowly avoided it. Like Susan, they may be naive about the dynamics of human relationships or out of touch with their feelings. They may be vulnerable because of loneliness or personal crisis. Like Susan, pastors can do something about the temptations. Sexual misconduct is completely preventable, if the clergyperson is self-aware and vigilant.

RISK FACTORS: THE TERRAIN
IN WHICH SEXUAL MISCONDUCT THRIVES

A key to preventing misconduct is understanding the risk factors.[4] Some risks are tied to characteristic roles of counselors and pastors. Pastors can reduce risks by taking preventive steps and becoming self-aware.

The Counseling Relationship

Counseling creates an environment conducive not only to emotional healing but also to sexual misconduct. Think about the counseling relationship. The parishioner often comes to the pastor in crisis, bringing vulnerability, unmet needs, and a desire to be heard. The pastor gives complete attention to the person, hearing, supporting, and even loving them. Counseling seeks to develop a deep emotional intimacy that is often the forerunner of sexual intimacy in our culture. A colleague of mine reminds seminarians that the things a good counselor does to establish a strong therapeutic relationship are the very same things people do to get someone in bed. The goals are different, but the techniques are similar. Given this dynamic and our natural drives, it is no surprise that parishioners are sometimes attracted to pastors and vice versa. Because of the potentially dangerous nature of this bond, pastors must be aware of the dynamics and the risks, take precautions to reduce them, and keep good boundaries.

The Distinctive Role of the Pastor

If this therapeutic role weren't hazardous enough, pastors face additional risks. While pastoral counseling in the parish may look like secular counseling, the pastoral role is distinctive. The boundaries between parishioner and pastor are more blurred. Normally, a therapist and client meet in the office for a set time to talk about the client's problems. They do not see each other outside of that setting. The therapist is not a part of the client's larger world. The client knows little of the therapist's world. The boundaries cannot be so clear-cut in the church. Good pastors see parishioners in many settings. Pastors and parishioners often know each other's families and friends and even attend the same social events. Good pastors are "fellow pilgrims" who talk about their struggles and witness to their faith. The pastoral role is simply different from the therapist's role. The lines are, of necessity, not as sharply drawn. This is a reality of ministry. Consequently, pastors must be all the more vigilant to avoid misconduct, to have clear structures of accountability, and to honor sexual boundaries.[5]

Other factors complicate the relationship. The pastor has power as leader, counselor, and representative of the church. This power can be misused to hurt others. In addition, pastors and churches are often more isolated and lack the structures of accountability found in most secular counseling. In one study, 61 percent of pastors spent "less than one hour a week talking with other pastors" (Minirth 1986, 86). And very little of that conversation is professional discussion of counseling. Christians can also be naive about the potential for evil among pastors. Pastors often lack both specialized training as counselors and ongoing professional supervision. The combination of power, isolation, naïveté, and lack of supervision raises the risks of misconduct and lowers the likelihood of accountability. Given these problems, pastoral caregivers have a great responsibility to work to avoid misconduct and to develop structures of accountability.

Clerical Bad Habits

Many clergypersons practice bad habits that can increase the risks of sexual misconduct. Pastors work longer hours and have greater job stress than most professionals. They isolate themselves, not seeking support from colleagues or intimacy with friends. Many pastors have high needs for praise and approval. They like to be needed. All of these factors can raise a pastor's risk. In addition, special circumstances can increase risks. A pastor in personal crisis is at much higher risk. The problem could be depression, work burnout, trouble with marriage or other significant relationships, or any other factor that leaves the pastor more vulnerable and needy. Pastors must remember these risk factors, so that they can work both to reduce them and to live faithfully amid the risks. In the face of the risks, clergy denial, do-nothingism, or naïveté is grossly irresponsible.

STEPS FOR PRACTICAL APPLICATION: PREVENTION, ACCOUNTABILITY, JUSTICE, AND CARE

These risks should heighten clergy awareness and vigilance. Clergy sexual misconduct is highly preventable. Pastors can work to protect themselves from misconduct and even the appearance of misconduct. They can develop procedures of accountability for themselves and others. They can compensate for risk factors and watch for warning signs. By following simple guidelines, pastors and other Christian leaders can reduce misconduct and hold more perpetrators accountable.[6]

Ground Rules

It is *never appropriate* to have sexual contact with parishioners.

• It is always the pastor's responsibility to keep the appropriate boundaries.
• Pastors and other leaders are also responsible for setting up and following procedures to hold pastors accountable.
• No pastor or church is free from the risks of misconduct. The only responsible path is to be aware of the problem, vigilant about prevention, and tenacious in following procedures of accountability. Ignorance, inaction, and denial are irresponsible.

Watching for Problems and Warning Signs

Susan and many other pastors have avoided misconduct by becoming attentive to the warning signs.

• *Be self-aware.* Know yourself. Know the risk factors and warning signs. Be even more cautious when you are particularly vulnerable.
• *Watch for signs that you are attracted to a parishioner.* Remember these questions: Do you take more care with your appearance when you expect to see this parishioner? Do you anticipate being with him or her? Do you find excuses to be around him or her? Do you set up appointments with this person that are outside the normal routine with other parishioners? Have you rescheduled appointments to be with this parishioner? Are you secretive about the level of interest and interaction? Would you be uncomfortable if others knew about the intensity of the relationship? Do you think about this parishioner a lot? Do you feel a heightened longing—sexual or emotional—in his or her presence? Are you much more aware of yourself sexually? Are you sharing more personal, intimate details than you normally would? Is there more touching, sexual innuendo, or mention of sex? Do you experience a mood change—elevation or agitation—around him or her? Do you have repeated sexual fantasies? If you are aware of an enduring attraction, move immediately to establish better boundaries. Limit your interactions to more public settings and stop sharing

intimate information. Stop fantasizing. Confess your attraction to a trustworthy colleague (but not to the parishioner). If the feelings are strong and enduring, do not counsel, but refer. Work to establish more appropriate avenues for intimacy in your own life.

• *Watch for signs that a parishioner might be attracted to you.* Is the person spending a lot of time with you, bringing gifts, finding excuses to drop by the office, being a little seductive, or bringing up intimate topics? The same questions that you asked of yourself also apply to the parishioner. If there seems to be improper attraction, be extremely clear about boundaries. There is no need to mention the attraction to the parishioner (talking about it can feed the intimacy). Simply remember the proper professional boundaries. A pastor can still be kind while maintaining more distance. If the attraction is extreme and enduring, consider referral. Read about the dynamics of transference and counter-transference so you can recognize them. Susan was able to act only when she began to pay attention to these signs.

• *Be especially vigilant in times of vulnerability.* If you are lonely, depressed, or in crisis, be all the more attentive to the preventative steps and warning signs. Keep stricter boundaries. Find an appropriate place to talk about problems and temptations. Susan recognized that her loneliness made her more vulnerable to misconduct.

• *Be particularly attentive if the parishioner is having marital problems, is sexually attracted, is in crisis, seems unstable, or is especially vulnerable.*

• *Whatever the attraction, whatever offers parishioners may make, it is always the pastor's responsibility to keep the boundaries.* It is never right to have sex with a parishioner. Whether or not a pastor recognizes the power and responsibility that comes with the position, it is there. The pastor must keep the appropriate boundaries.

Steps for Prevention: The Individual Clergyperson

Establish procedures of accountability for yourself. Make rules about interactions with others. Avoid sexualizing interactions with staff and church members (for example, by making offensive jokes or comments). Watch for warning signs. Do not get carried away with sexual fantasies about church members and staff. Find responsible ways to be intimate with others.

Be cautious and self-aware when forming close friendships with parishioners. Find people who are healthy and mature. Dual relationships carry risks. Know the risks and respond accordingly.

Find a trustworthy confessor to talk with when you are attracted to someone or when facing other problems. Devise a plan to avoid misconduct. Make sure the confessor shares your moral assumptions about faithfulness and sexual boundaries and will also hold you accountable.

If you counsel parishioners, have regular supervision with a licensed supervisor. Consider asking the church to pay for it.

Set up your office and counseling procedures to protect yourself from misconduct or even the appearance of misconduct. Counsel in your office only when other people are in the building. Leave your door unlocked. Consider getting rid of blinds or curtains. Have a window put in the office door and position your chair where you (but not the parishioner) can be seen at any time.

If you need to meet a parishioner outside the office, find a public place. If a parishioner comes to your home, make sure someone else (a spouse or trusted church member) is in the next room, the blinds are open, and the doors are closed (for the privacy of the parishioner) but unlocked.

Be wary of home visits or trips where you are alone with a parishioner. If you need to visit individuals at their homes and have reason to be uncomfortable, take another parishioner with you.

If a situation feels wrong or strange, trust your gut instincts and keep very strict boundaries. If appropriate, refer.

If you are uncomfortable or sense that the other person is uncomfortable, refrain from touch. In private settings, be particularly cautious. Whatever setting, follow their lead on whether to shake hands or hug. When hugging, use a side hug, so that the shoulders touch instead of frontal hugs where the chests touch. If you lean in a little, the hips also don't touch. Be sensitive without overdoing it. I recently shook hands with an elderly widow, who then said, "I sure do like hugs, but I don't like to initiate them." So I gave her a big bear hug.

Be cautious about some discussions of sex. Of course, in Sunday school discussions or counseling, it is sometimes appropriate. But be thoughtful.

Whatever your sexual orientation and gender, take precautions with men and women. Just because you are not attracted to them does not mean they are not attracted to you. Also, the purpose of these steps is to avoid not only misconduct but also the appearance of misconduct.

Take care of yourself. Find Sabbath time. Pray. Cultivate ways to relax and relieve stress. Develop interests outside the parish. Find responsible channels for intimacy. If married, build a strong relationship with your spouse. Married or single, build strong relationships with friends.

Know and follow the procedures of your denomination or church.

Know that you cannot avoid all risks in a fallen world. While taking these precautions seriously, try not to become so cautious and paranoid that you are no longer open to parishioners. Pastors can't wall themselves up in fortresses. Try not to lose the freedom that comes with grace. Be aware of all the risks and suggestions, then risk being a pastor.

Responding to Clergy Sexual Misconduct

If you know of a pastor who is guilty of sexual misconduct, pursue the matter immediately. You may, on scriptural grounds, choose to go directly to the pastor for a personal discussion. If you do, take someone with you. And don't let it stop there. Use the official procedures of your church or denomination to pursue the matter. Know the laws of your state and denomination. Involve a trustworthy person who has power. Honor confidentiality. Document everything.

If you face false charges of sexual misconduct, find a lawyer and get emotional support from trustworthy friends and family. Use the established procedures. If charges are coming, get the procedure going quickly. Established procedures usually are more confidential than letting rumors fly. Have an advocate represent you. Talk to your supervisors and denominational officials. If you are not on good terms with them, make sure you involve another leader who has power and is in your corner. Remember that even genuine charges are hard to prove. If you are innocent, it is highly unlikely that you will be found guilty. Even so, know that you cannot control what other people believe. Trust the process. Trust in God. In the meantime, protect your backside and pray like mad.

If you are guilty of sexual misconduct, confess to the appropriate person in your denomination or church and seek help for yourself and your family. If you are a predator, get out of ministry. Find other work that has lower risks for you and those you work with. Do what you can to make things a little easier for those you have wronged. You cannot make up for the hurt you have caused. You cannot undo your sin. But you can choose now to act with integrity. Repent, change your life, and take the consequences. If Ben could have left ministry sooner, many people, including his own family, could have been saved much grief.

Remember the sacred nature of your calling and the responsibilities that come with it. Call on God and fellow Christians to support you in being faithful.

Remember that pastors are responsible not only for refraining from miscon-duct but also for setting up and following structures of accountability for themselves and other pastors.

Taking Steps for Prevention and Accountability in the Church

Establish policies and procedures to address sexual misconduct in your church and denomination. Ask at a denominational office about stan-dard procedures. Publicize the procedures.

- *Implement all policies and procedures to the letter.*
- *Ask a few trustworthy parishioners to be trained as contact persons in case problems develop.* Make their names public.
- *Use the steps of establishing and explaining the procedures as an edu-cational tool for administrative committees and the entire congregation.*
- *Address the issue openly (in worship, sermons, Sunday school classes, or newsletters), so that the congregation will be more ready if problems develop and parishioners will know that they can safely talk about any abuse.*
- *Set up community conversation times if appropriate.* Remember that some people will not want to talk about this issue. Don't push them. Just make sure the policy is known and that people have opportuni-ties to talk about it.
- *Hold a workshop on sexual abuse and boundaries for all staff and pri-mary church volunteers (especially children and youth workers).*
- *Take particular care to screen, train, and supervise children and youth workers.* Establish a policy so that no one is alone with an individual young person except in public places.
- *If you suspect that children are being abused, you must report to the appropriate agency immediately.*
- *Find out about community agencies specializing in sexual abuse (abuse counselors, rape crisis centers, shelters, and so forth).* Have infor-mation about these resources available in church offices and on church bulletin boards.
- *Help to change laws and society so that the vulnerable will be protected and abusers held accountable.*

Pastoral Care With Survivors

Be present, listen, and accept the reality of their pain. Be cautious about touch. Reassure them of your support. Refer to counselors who special-ize in sexual abuse. Help survivors make the connection with the referral and support groups. Continue to check in with them after the referral is made. Don't rush them to get over their anger or to forgive. Forgiveness takes time and justice. Don't challenge the person to prove the charges. The investigation of charges should be a different task undertaken by a separate body.

Explain the process of investigation and charges to parishioners. If they choose to file charges, guide them through the process. If your church has persons designated to hear complaints, arrange for survivors to meet with one of them. Help a survivor to find others who can be advocates through the process. Reassure him or her that you will continue to offer support.

Follow your denomination's procedure for reporting abuse. Even if the parishioner does not want to file a formal grievance, you may be required to report. According to some state laws and most church policies, Karl could be charged for failing to report. If you have no procedure, call the central office of a larger denomination in your area. (Most mainline denominations have policies and extensive resources.) Find support for yourself. Leonard, for example, talked with his counseling supervisor.

Pastoral Care With Those Accused:
Before Being Found Guilty or Not Guilty

A fair policy is a godsend to someone falsely accused. Have a policy in place that can deal with these problems fairly and professionally. Use it. If there are questions of abuse of children or youth, report the suspicions immediately to the appropriate agency. Insist that the accused stay away from the complainant and other vulnerable people. Listen to the person. Do not assume that he or she is guilty. Offer care, but don't rush to assume innocence either. Provide support for the family members of the alleged perpetrator (and for the complainants and their families).

Pastoral Care With a Pastor Found Guilty

Remember that true justice and love will work to hold perpetrators accountable. Be willing to confront. Encourage perpetrators to get long-term therapy. Look for referrals to counselors and groups specializing in sexual abuse. Remember that the success or "cure" rate is abysmally low. So no matter what treatment is given, protect others from further abuse. Limit the perpetrator's access to the vulnerable. Expect to hear extraordinary excuses and self-justification. Don't smooth things over or rush to forgiveness. Follow all policies and procedures to the letter. Offer care and compassion to the families of the perpetrator and the survivor. When possible, get the perpetrator out of ordained ministry. Also remember to seek out and support the families of guilty pastors.

Pastoral Care With Someone Falsely Accused

If someone has been accused and the charges are shown to be without foundation, help the person and families deal with the grief, anger, and frustration. Suggest counseling. Work to clear the person's name and, when possible, to undo any harm to their ability to work or to be involved in community. Go out of your way to make sure that the person is invited to church events and welcomed. Be a catalyst for helping the community reestablish relationship with this person. If, however, the person was found "not guilty" on a technicality, but you still have good reason to believe he or she is actually guilty, watch the person like a hawk and protect the vulnerable.

WHAT THEN SHALL WE DO?: A RETURN TO THE CASES

Keeping these guidelines in mind and remembering the steps of moral guidance outlined in chapter 2, let's return to the three cases. How might pastors respond if they were guiding Karl, Leonard, Ben, or Susan? In cases like these, pastors have a professional and moral responsibility to be direct and to insist that the proper procedures be followed. With clergy sexual misconduct (in contrast to some other ethical problems), responsible pastors cannot enter into an extended series of conversations about whether or not misconduct should be stopped. How might a good pastor respond?

If Karl called a fellow pastor as soon as he heard about the original accusation, what might the pastor say? The pastor could affirm Karl's decision to seek guidance about the matter and stress his responsibility to report the charge. The pastor might say:

> Karl, you are doing the right thing to talk with someone about the accusation. It must have been tempting to ignore it and hope it would go away. Let's look at the procedures for our denomination and talk through our options. . . . Given our options, what should we do now?

Knowing about the charges, both Karl and the fellow pastor now have an obligation to act responsibly. If more senior to Karl, the fellow pastor can take the greater responsibility in making the decisions, setting up the meeting with the church officials, and helping protect Karl from political fallout. If Karl or the fellow pastor has little power in the denomination, they should seek out someone who has more power.

If Leonard brings his case to a fellow pastor, the pastor will quickly realize that he is following all the procedures and doing everything he can to stop the abuse and hold Ben accountable. Once the pastor is sure that Leonard is acting responsibly, the primary task is to support Leonard, listen to his frustrations, and offer counsel where appropriate.

The role is not so simple with Ben. A pastor would be morally obligated to tell Ben that his misconduct is not acceptable. Because of the gravity of the behavior, the pastor can take a direct, confrontational approach, saying something like this:

> As a fellow pastor, I have a responsibility to tell you that what you have done is morally wrong. You have abused your calling and the very people placed in your care. It is my responsibility to do everything I can to stop the misconduct and to hold you accountable.

In another approach, the pastor could begin by asking morally leading questions to try to get Ben to come to that conclusion himself. The pastor could ask, "What are the consequences of your abusive behavior for this person and the church? Is having sexual intercourse with a parishioner in keeping with your sacred call by God?" Remember that the point is not to hear Ben's answers or opinions, but to help him come to the truth. In most situations the perpetrator either already knows that the behavior is wrong or is in such denial that no questions, no matter how thoughtful, will evoke responsibility. If the leading questions approach is taken, the pastor must still directly confront the perpetrator.

The pastor may also need to help Ben or another perpetrator do some moral brush clearing. Perpetrators are remarkably adept at distracting and rationalizing. If Ben focuses on something else, perhaps the unhappiness of his marriage, the pastor could simply say:

> I see that you are unhappy in your marriage. Perhaps you and Carol might begin marriage counseling. But the main issue you and I have to deal with right now is not your marital problems, but the sexual misconduct. Let's keep the focus on the misconduct.

The pastor can also watch for overlooked or hidden features. The pastor could ask Ben directly and firmly, "Are you having sex with her? Have you had sex or any romantic involvement with other parishioners? Is there anything else that you are not telling me?"

The pastor can also help Ben explore the options in a direct and even confrontational way. The pastor could say:

> Thinking about what you've told me and about the policies of our church, I see several options. You can either stop the abuse and go directly to the

authorities (a bishop, a lay committee, a denominational official), confessing what you have done and hoping that they will be lenient. Or you can choose to do nothing, in which case, I will immediately initiate the denominational procedures for investigation. Which will it be?

With a repeated perpetrator like Ben, the first task is taking immediate action to protect the people of the church. If the conversations with him are also beneficial, that is fine. But don't be sidetracked into focusing your energies on changing the perpetrator. Instead, focus on protecting the people. Don't be fooled by the perpetrator's excuses and assurances. Holding perpetrators accountable is best not only for the church, but also for the perpetrators. As Christians, we believe that true repentance and a change of behavior are crucial to our relationship with God. Be direct for the people's sake and for the perpetrator's sake. Cheap grace serves nothing.

With someone like Susan, the task is easier. Because there hasn't been any actual misconduct, the conversation is preventive. Also, the fact that Susan has sought the pastor out is a sign that she is aware and is taking responsibility. A first step is to acknowledge and affirm this. A pastor could say:

> The fact that you came to talk with me says that you know there is a problem and want to be responsible. That is the most important step in prevention.

The pastor then has four additional tasks. First, to help Susan devise a plan for reestablishing boundaries with Dale and preventing misconduct, the pastor could say, "You want to avoid misconduct and reestablish boundaries. What immediate steps can you take? Here's a pen. Why don't you write them down?" The pastor can offer suggestions for the list. Second, the pastor can help Susan to think about the larger problems in her own life that may have placed her at greater risk for misconduct and also to devise strategies to address those problems.

> In my experience, when pastors are tempted by misconduct, there are usually other stresses and unhealthy patterns in their lives that place them at higher risk. Can you think of things going on in your life that have made you more vulnerable to misconduct? . . . I sense that you want to do something about these problems that may have put you at a higher risk for misconduct. What immediate steps might you take? Could you add those to the list?

Third, Susan and the pastor can negotiate an accountability covenant. The pastor could say:

> In my experience, a key step in avoiding misconduct is to have a fixed, predetermined covenant of accountability with another person to hold us

accountable. I would like us to develop a plan that incorporates the ideas that you've had for responding to the problems. We could set up a schedule to talk regularly and we could agree that whenever a problem arises, you'll call me. Here are my telephone and pager numbers. Perhaps we could plan to talk in a few days and then meet again next Wednesday to see how things are coming with the strategies and changes that you've listed today.

Fourth, the pastor can also summarize the conversation in a way that reviews the strategies, normalizes the problem, and affirms Susan's response without taking away from the gravity of any potential for misconduct.

> Before we close, I want to add that you are facing a temptation that is a normal part of ministry. Pastors have the same emotional and physical needs as any other person. The truth is, most pastors feel tempted at some point. The crucial thing is not whether pastors are tempted, but what they do when they are tempted. You are doing exactly what a responsible pastor should do—recognizing the problem, seeking out help, devising strategies to work with Dale and to change your own lifestyle, and agreeing to an accountability covenant. You are doing the right things that will help you continue to be a faithful pastor. And I am committed to doing everything I can to help you remain faithful and to hold you accountable to your sacred calling. As fellow pastors, you and I are in this struggle together.

Finally, the pastor can pray with Susan. While pastors often pray for others, they rarely have another pastor pray for them. The prayer could ask for support and guidance as Susan works to remain faithful to her calling.

These suggestions assume, of course, that there has been no misconduct and that there is no immediate danger of misconduct. If a pastor believes that misconduct has occurred or is imminent, conversations will need to be more direct and confrontational. In all of these cases, responsible pastors should act swiftly and directly to respond to misconduct or even the possibility of misconduct.

WHAT'S OUR PROBLEM?: A THEOLOGY FOR THE MINISTRY OF PASTORAL CARE

Whenever a pastor is accused of sexual misconduct, no matter how massive the evidence, odd things happen. People say something like this: "I don't believe it. He's too good a man." What's so strange about this phenomenon is not that Christians think the accused is a good person, but that they are surprised that good people sin. When Christians deny that a good person can fall, I have to wonder whether they learned about human nature from Scriptures and life or from Hallmark® cards and *Mr. Rogers' Neighborhood*? It isn't always "a wonderful day in the neighborhood." We can count on the fact that both pastors and parishioners will sin. Given that reality, we should plan for sin, establishing structures for prevention and accountability.

Throughout this work, I have claimed that Christians in our culture need both a higher and lower view of many parts of our daily life. We need a higher and lower view of marriage, sexuality, and work. On the higher side of work, for example, we need to recognize that work is sacred because God has called us to it. On the lower side, we need to not romanticize the tasks. They bring both joy and sorrow. They will not meet all our needs or bring ultimate fulfillment. We also need a more realistic account of the sin that pervades human activities. In the face of this realistic accounting, we take on the difficult tasks because we are called.

The move to promote both higher and lower views of marriage and work is carried into this discussion of sexual misconduct and, more important, into our reflections about the calling of pastoral ministry and the tasks of moral guidance. In the end, we need both a higher and lower view of ordained ministry. We need a chastened idealism and a hopeful realism. Pastors and parishioners expect too much of ordained ministers, romanticizing both the role and person. A more realistic view of pastors and ministry would plan for sin, prompting Christians to set up procedures to protect pastors and parishioners from pastors and parishioners. Pastors also need a more realistic view of their own jobs. Pastors, particularly new ones, often expect ministers to be holy and the church to be pure. The problem with churches is that they are peopled and guided by sinful humans. Leading a church can bring as much trouble as it brings blessings.

Ordained ministry is no more free from toil, sin, or impermanence than other jobs. Remember the words of Ecclesiastes, "All is vanity." The work of ordained ministry, no matter how grand, will be swept away by the current of time. With the "preacher" of Ecclesiastes, all we can do is recognize its impermanence and rejoice in our labor. It is what God has given us to do. We need to be more realistic about the vocation of ordained ministry.

The church also needs a higher view of pastoral ministry. Sure, pastors are sinners like everybody else, but they are sinners with greater responsibility. Being a pastor may be just another job, but it is a job with high stakes. A higher and lower view of the pastorate recognizes both the sacred calling and terrible risks of ministry. Because pastors are given responsibility for the care of others, they bear greater responsibility for misleading them. Pastors would do well to remember the words in Ezekiel declaring God's judgment on false shepherds who care only for themselves, who foul the sheep's water with their feet, and who do nothing when the sheep are "food for all the wild animals" (34:8). "Thus says the Lord God, I am against the shepherds; and I will demand my sheep at their hand, and put a stop to their feeding the sheep; no longer shall the shepherds feed themselves. I will rescue my sheep from their mouths, so that they may not be food for them" (34:10).

Condemnation falls not only on those who actively harm the sheep, but also on those who do nothing when the sheep are "food for all the wild animals" (34:8) and preyed upon for "lack of a shepherd." A new realism and idealism about ministry calls not only for a condemnation of the shepherd's misconduct and the wolf's violence, but also of the failure of other shepherds to protect the sheep. That charge could apply not only to those who fail to report misconduct (like Karl), but to all pastors and other Christian leaders who have failed to do everything in their power to protect the sheep, whether from sexual misconduct or any other danger. That indictment includes me and many others.

With a renewed realism, pastors recognize the stark realities of misconduct and the responsibility to work for prevention and accountability. With a renewed idealism, pastors remind themselves and others of their high calling. They expect great things. As idealists, they expect the best. As realists, they plan for the worst. They are "wise as serpents and innocent as doves" (Matt. 10:16).

These reflections apply not only to the problem of sexual misconduct and the general tasks of ordained ministry. They also apply to the ministry of moral guidance. Moral guides are given a tough job. Moral guidance carries all the dangers of any other part of ministry. Pastors can be too lax or too demanding. They can fail for lack of knowledge, lack of courage, lack of patience, or lack of love. Though they sometimes get it right, they just as often get it wrong. Moral guidance is a high-stakes business.

With high expectations for the vocation of ministry and low expectations considering the realities of human sin and limits, guides are in a tough spot. It is no wonder that many hesitate. It is no wonder that Gregory Nazianzen, John Chrysostom, and so many others tried to run away. In the end, what can guides do but joyfully obey the call and trust in God? How can moral guides respond but to echo the fourth-century prayer of Gregory Nazianzen? "May the God of peace . . . hold me by my right hand and guide me . . . Who is a Shepherd to shepherds and a Guide to guides" (1995, 227).

CONCLUSION

This book tells only one small part of the story. Yes, Christian moral guidance is about pastors working with parishioners in pastoral care and counseling—providing strategies, talking about rules, and making good choices. But moral guidance is more than that. Ultimately, moral guidance is a communal act of love. It is a labor of the body of Christ in the world.

Moral guidance matters because goodness and virtue must be nourished, guided, and tended. We learn to be good in the company of fellow pilgrims. We are led by the words of practiced travelers and by the steps of those who have gone before us. We are taught by their guidance and example, in both moral goodness and failure. Through the fragile bonds of Christian community—the body of Christ in the world—we love each other not to death, but to life. We love each other into goodness and virtue. Moral guidance is a participation in love. Moral pilgrimage is a quest of love.

In the introduction, I told a story about an official pilgrim guide who gave not guidance but a brush-off. I close with another pilgrimage story about exquisite guidance from an unexpected quarter—about the power of ordinary acts of love.

A few summers ago, my husband and I traveled the pilgrimage route of Saint James across northern Spain. We stopped in the small town of Najera where the kings and queens of Navarre once ruled and now lie buried. In the crypt of the town church, we found the tombs and were searching for one particularly fine sarcophagus. Because we do not know a fine sarcophagus from a sorry one, we looked for someone who could tell us, and we found a tiny, old woman, her frame bent from fifty years tending the crypt. She was feather-dusting each tomb with one hand and caressing it with the other. On the top of each tomb lay a life-size carving of the body buried within. Working down the line of tombs, often stretching up to reach the reclining figures of stone, she dusted and caressed them, touching their faces, telling us gently about each king and each queen as if she had known them and served them. And I suppose she had.

When we stood before the prize sarcophagus, she stopped her work and began talking louder and faster, jabbing the air with her feather duster. She was mad because the Metropolitan Museum of Art wanted to take her sarcophagus to New York City. They had offered to pay a huge amount. They had raised the offer several times. But no matter how high the bid, she was against it. In the Spanish of the ancients, she told us, "They do not know its value. They would not care for it." She leaned in close, whispering. "Besides, maybe they would drop it. Break it to pieces. No, it should stay here, where I can care for it." She stroked the tomb with her feather duster, touched the stone, sighed before its beauty.

Now her logic struck me as odd. Surely the curators of the Metropolitan would know the value of the piece and would care for it. They would not drop it. They would not break it into pieces. They would even insure it. And yet . . . they would probably not love it or sigh before its beauty. They would surely not feather-dust and caress it.

The old woman's love for this beautiful thing reminded us of a favorite passage from Erazim Kohak, a Czech philosopher, on the distinction between possessing things and belonging to them.

> Though humans may need to formalize having as possessing, the living truth of having is belonging, the bond of love and respect which grows between one being and another in the course of the seasons. The claim to having is as strong as all the love and care a person gives, and only that strong. . . . Without love [and care] the claim to having becomes void. Loveless having remains illegitimate, a theft. . . . Humans are justified by the power of their love to bring the world alive, to give things the love, care and use they need for their fulfillment. . . . That is not a matter of taking possession of the world but of making it our own in a bond of mutual belonging, of taking the world with us from the flow of temporality into eternity (Kohak 1984, 107–8).

Loveless having is "illegitimate, a theft." Belonging in love is life and power. Through love and care, tending and belonging, we "bring the world" and ourselves "alive." By the homely means of feather-dusting and caressing, we carry all "from the flow of temporality into eternity." The power of love makes the finite infinite, the fleeting eternal, the temporal enduring.

There is another way of seeing this matter, a way that looks ultimately not to the enduring but to the fragile, not to the eternal but to the finite. Martha Nussbaum, quoted at the beginning of this book, turns to Greek tragedy and moral philosophy to ask how the flourishing of human character, the tending of human virtue and excellence are intimately tied to that which is finite and fragile. She quotes the Greek poet Pindar: "But human excellence grows like a vine tree, fed by the green dew, raised up, among wise men [sic] and just, to the liquid sky." Nussbaum reflects:

> So Pindar displays a problem that lies at the heart of Greek thought about the good life for a human being. . . . The excellence of the good person, he

writes, is like a young plant: something growing in the world, slender, fragile, in constant need of food from without. . . . It needs fostering weather . . . as well as the care of concerned and intelligent keepers, for its continued health and full perfection. So, the poet suggests, do we. . . . The poem's next lines are, "We have all kinds of needs for those we love: most of all in hardships, but joy, too, strains to track down eyes that it can trust." Our openness to fortune and our sense of value, here again, both render us dependent on what is outside of us . . . something that only another can provide . . . And all these needs for all these things that we do not humanly control are pertinent, clearly, not only to feelings of contentment or happiness. What the external nourishes and even helps to constitute is excellence or human worth itself (Nussbaum 1986, 1).

If Nussbaum and Pindar are right, then goodness and virtue must be tended. Our character depends on it. Our virtue relies on things that are vulnerable, even fragile. Chief among these is human community. We, too, "strain to track down eyes that [we] can trust." For Pindar and Nussbaum, the good life, human happiness or blessedness, is not the isolated life. It is not the secure life, protected from the fragile world. The abundant life is found in the fullness of community, of tender human relationships of love and care, belonging and guidance. And these relationships, so central to the growth and tending of human character and excellence, are of necessity fragile. Conflicts arise, misunderstandings abound, communities fragment, friends die, and perhaps most often, relationships untended lose their vitality, their power, their life. Our good—our moral character and virtue—is dependent on that which is fragile and finite, on relationships that demand love and guidance, tending and attention, feather-dusting and caressing.

We find here two very different ways of looking at the world. In the first, the fleeting is made eternal, the fragile carried to eternity by the extraordinary power of human love; *therefore, we must love*. In the second, our lives and our virtue are unavoidably fragile, always dependent on the exquisite tenderness of fleeting human love; *therefore, we must love*. For all their ancient differences, both visions—idealism and realism—share a call to love and guidance, tending and attention, feather-dusting and caressing.

What does all of this have to do with us—moral guides, pastoral caregivers, and members of the body of Christ? It is in feather-dusting and caressing that we bring the world and ourselves alive. Only in tending and loving, guiding and caring can we nurture the tender shoots of human goodness and virtue. Our good, our virtue, and our character are shaped in community—in the fragile community of any parish, and in the eternal community of the mystical body of Christ. Loveless having remains "illegitimate, a theft." Belonging in love is life and power. Only through true belonging, feather-dusting and caressing, guiding and tending do we bring ourselves and our world alive. Our character and our virtue depend on these vulnerable and fragile relationships. Do we tend the Body of Christ? Do we value it, care for it, feather-dust and caress it? Do we love and guide its members? Do we struggle faithfully with fellow pilgrims? In our labor and our guidance, do we bring the world and each other alive?

Our character is dependent on the fragile care of other finite creatures and on the leading of all-too-human guides. But, for Christians, that is not the whole story. As we love, we participate in eternity, in the perfection of God's love in the world. As we guide, we are led and forgiven by the one who is the Guide to guides. In the end, we can rejoice, knowing that our souls are tended and led not only by other creatures, but by our Creator. As we love and care for each other, we travel toward and participate in God's love. And in those ordinary human moments of love, the goodness of fragile creatures is tended and led by God's enduring love— a love that carries us "from the flow of temporality into eternity." Loving moral guidance is a participation in God's love. It is a labor of the body of Christ in the world.

> Beloved, let us love one another, because love is from God; everyone who loves is born of God and knows God. Whoever does not love does not know God, for God is love. . . . Beloved, since God loved us so much, we also ought to love one another. No one has ever seen God; if we love one another, God lives in us, and his love is perfected in us. By this we know that we abide in him and he in us, because he has given us of his Spirit. . . . God is love, and those who abide in love abide in God, and God abides in them. Love has been perfected among us in this: that we may have boldness on the day of judgment, because as he is, so are we in this world (1 John 4:7-17).

NOTES

Introduction

1. In most cases throughout this book, names and identifying details have been changed to guard the privacy of the people described.

2. For further background on the main points of this section, see Browning 1983 and 1986; Burck 1991; Poling 1991; Stone 1996; and Noyce 1987. I have been especially influenced by the work of Don Browning.

3. Note the difficulties with the work of Capps (1995) and others who focus on desire without giving it clear moral content or ultimate end. A Christian ethic asks about and evaluates the ultimate object or end of one's desire and hope. Capps and others seem to suggest that individuals should define their own ends or desires. They do not offer guidance about how one judges among ends and desires. This is a liberal individualist argument, not a Christian one. In spite of the tendency in pastoral care to shy away from moral guidance, several scholars call for pastors to embrace their role as moral counselor (Browning 1976, Noyce 1987, and Poling 1991).

4. Clergy professional ethics, a more recent movement in the field, does apply more directly to the parish (Lebacqz 1985; Gula 1996; Trull and Carter 1993; and Wiest and Smith 1990). These texts center on the ethics of pastors and particular acts of ministry. They cover important issues such as clergy misconduct, relationships with colleagues, and abuses of power, but overlook the pastor's role as guide.

5. For a more extensive discussion of realism, see Miles (1995). I have been influenced by the work of Lovin (1995) and Niebuhr (1941).

2. Being Doers of the Word

1. See Weiner-Davis 1992; de Shazer 1985; and O'Hanlon and Weiner-Davis 1989. Stone (1993 and 1994) has a similar approach, applying techniques of crisis counseling and short-term therapies to pastoral care. My analysis has also been influenced by Schlessinger (1995 and 1996).

3. Good and Faithful Servants

1. Though overwork is a critical problem among parishioners and is the focus of this chapter, it is not the only problem. For some in our culture, the problem is not too much work but too little. In addition, in some cases, the scandal of American unemployment and underpay is worsened by individual reluctance to work and social failure to train for work or to provide jobs. While these

are significant problems, they are not the primary focus of this chapter. This chapter centers primarily on the issues of working people—whether blue-collar or white-collar, pink-collar, or clerical-collar. Because the other questions are crucial not only for policymakers but also pastoral caregivers, they merit greater attention than they could be given here.

2. In the last several years, there have been many studies on work. One of the most commonly cited (and the basis for most of the statistics in this chapter) is the study by Harvard economist Juliet Schor (1993). Hochschild's recent work (1997) has also attracted considerable attention with the media. For the other side of the argument, see Peyser 1997; Clark 1996; Height 1997; and Godbey and Robinson 1995. Other studies of work that are significant to my analysis include Arendt 1958; Bielski 1996; Ehrenreich 1990; Ellul 1974; Fassel 1990; Fox 1994; Heschel 1951; Hochschild 1989 and 1997b; Killinger 1991; Linder 1970; Minirth, Hawkins, Meier, and Flournoy 1986; Noyce 1987, chapter 8; Oates 1971; Raines and Day-Lower 1986; Rifkin 1995; Ryken 1995; Shapiro 1997; Terkel 1972; Ventura 1995; Volf 1991; Walljasper 1997; Calhoun 1954; and Clarke 1995.

3. This history is widely known. I relied on primary sources as well as surveys by Arendt 1958; Ryken 1995; Calhoun 1954; Clarke 1995; and Ellul 1974.

4. I Am My Beloved's and My Beloved Is Mine

1. Quoted by Roland Bainton (1957, 82).

2. These statistics are widely cited. I have drawn most heavily from Gallagher 1996; Whitehead 1997; and Galston 1996. See the bibliography for further references.

3. See, for example, Furstenburg and Cherlin (1991) and Wallerstein and Blakeslee (1989). These studies and others have spawned a lively popular debate. See Zinsmeister 1997; Adelson 1996; Shapiro 1997; Gallagher 1996; Whitehead 1997; etc.

4. See, for example, Nelson 1992, McFague 1993, Ruether 1992, and Fox 1983.

5. This realism stands in sharp contrast to some recent church statements that over-romanticize sexuality, forgetting the other side—the chaos, sin, and distortion. This romantic stance is poorly prepared to deal with the distortion in some sexual desires and practices.

5. Keeping Watch over the Shepherds by Day and Night

1. For an examination of other aspects of clergy ethics, see my forthcoming work *A Charge to Keep: Ethics and Etiquette in the Ordinary Practices of Parish Ministry* (Nashville: Abingdon Press). Other works addressing clergy ethics include Trull and Carter 1993; Gula 1996; Wiest and Smith 1990; and Lebacqz 1985.

2. For resources on clergy sexual misconduct, see Fortune 1989; Lebacqz and Barton 1991; Gula 1996, 91–116; Berry, 1992; Fortune 1992; Grenz and Bell 1995; Trull and Carter 1993, 80–93; and Chaffee 1997, 185–208. This chapter

draws from these sources and my own experience, as well as from conversations with clergy and laity, documents from United Methodist agencies and conferences, and several seminary workshops on clergy sexual misconduct led by JoAnn and John Miles.

3. These statistics originated with a study of 300 pastors (Blackmon 1984). Blackmon's study and several others found similar statistics that are quoted widely throughout the literature. See Blackmon and Hart 1990, 39; Trull and Carter 1993, 80–82; Grenz and Bell 1995, 22–23; and Fortune 1992, 14.

4. The study of risk factors by Balswick and Thorburn (1991) is the most widely known. See also Trull and Carter 1993, 80–86; Fortune 1989, 103–6; Blackmon and Hart 1990; Lebacqz and Barton 1991; Grenz and Bell 1995, 37–61; and Chaffee 1997, 185–208.

5. For a heated debate on the nature of boundaries in counseling, see Heyward and Fortune 1994.

6. Most studies and workshops on clergy sexual misconduct center on prevention. The information here is drawn from conversations with pastors and workshop leaders as well as the following resources: Gula 1996, 107–16; Chaffee 1997, 185–208; Trull and Carter 1993, 86–88; Blackmon and Hart 1990, 48; Lebacqz and Barton 1991; Fortune 1989; Balswick and Thorburn 1991; and Grenz and Bell 1995, 129–47.

BIBLIOGRAPHY

Adelson, J. 1996. Splitting up. *Commentary* 102(3) (September): 63–66.

Ambrose. 1995. *On the duties of the clergy.* Trans. H. de Romestin. Vol. 10 of A Select Library of the Nicene and Post-Nicene Fathers of the Christian Church, 2d ser., ed. Henry Wace and Philip Schaff, 1–89. Peabody, Mass.: Hendrickson Publishers.

Anderson, H. 1984. *The family and pastoral care.* Philadelphia: Fortress Press.

Aquinas, T. 1952. Whether religious are bound by manual labour? In *Summa Theologiae* III. Great Books of the Western World, vol. 20, ed. R. M. Hutchins, 666–69. Chicago: Encyclopedia Britannica Inc.

Arendt, H. 1958. *The human condition.* Chicago: Doubleday Anchor Books.

Bainton, R. 1957. *What Christianity says about sex, love and marriage.* New York: Association Press.

Balswick, J., and J. Thorburn. 1991. How ministers deal with sexual temptation. *Pastoral Psychology* 39:277–86.

Bellah, R., R. Madsen, W. Sullivan, A. Swidler, and S. Tipton. 1985. *Habits of the heart: Individualism and commitment in American life.* Berkeley: University of California.

Berkley, J. D. 1989. *Called into crisis: The nine great challenges of pastoral care.* Carol Stream, Ill.: Word Publishing.

Berry, J. 1992. *Lead us not into temptation.* New York: Doubleday.

Bielski, V. 1996. Our magnificent obsession. *The Family Therapy Networker* 20(2) (March/April): 22–35.

Blackmon, R. A. 1984. The hazards of ministry. Ph.D. diss., Fuller Theological Seminary.

Blackmon R. A., and A. D. Hart. 1990. Personal growth for clergy. In *Clergy assessment and career development,* ed. A. Hunt, J. E. Hinkle, and H. N. Malony. Nashville: Abingdon Press.

Bondi, R. 1989. *Leading God's people: Ethics for the practice of ministry.* Nashville: Abingdon Press.

Boyajian, J., ed. 1984. *Ethical issues in the practice of pastoral ministry.* Minneapolis: United Theological Seminary of the Twin Cities.

Browning, D. 1976. *The moral context of pastoral care.* Philadelphia: Fortress Press.

———. 1983. *Religious ethics and pastoral care.* Philadelphia: Fortress Press.

———. 1986. Ethical problems in counseling. In *The Westminster dictionary of Christian ethics,* ed. James F. Childress and John Macquarrie. Philadelphia: Westminster Press.

Burck, J. R. 1991. Pastoral care and ethics. In *Clergy ethics in a changing society: Mapping the terrain,* ed. James Wind, Russell Burck, Paul Camenisch, and Dennis McCann, 178–97. Louisville, Ky.: Westminster/John Knox Press.

Calhoun, R. L. 1954. Work and vocation in Christian history. In *Work and vocation: A Christian discussion,* ed. J. O. Nelson, 82–115. New York: Harper & Brothers.

Calvin, J. 1960. The Lord's calling a basis of our way of life. In *Institutes of the Christian religion,* bk. 3, 10.6. The Library of Christian Classics, vol. 20, ed. J. T. Niell, 724–25. Philadelphia: Westminster Press.

Campbell, D. 1982. *Doctors, lawyers, ministers: Christian ethics in professional practice.* Nashville: Abingdon Press.

Capps, D. 1995. *Agents of hope: A pastoral psychology.* Minneapolis: Fortress Press.

Chaffee, P. 1997. *Accountable leadership.* San Francisco: Jossey-Bass Publishers.

Chaucer, G. 1952. *Canterbury tales.* Great Books of the Western World, vol. 22, ed. R. M. Hutchins. Chicago: Encyclopedia Britannica, Inc.

Childress, J. F., and J. Macquarrie, eds. 1986. *The Westminster dictionary of Christian ethics.* Philadelphia: Westminster Press.

Chrysostom, J. 1984. *Six books on the priesthood.* Trans. Graham Neville. Crestwood, N.Y.: St. Vladimir's Seminary Press.

Clark, K. 1996. Do you really work more? *Fortune* 133(8) (April 29): 66–68.

Clarke, P. 1995. Work. In *Dictionary of ethics, theology, and society,* ed. P. Clarke and A. Linsey. New York: Routledge Press.

Clebsch, W., and C. Jaekle. 1964. *Pastoral care in historical perspective.* Englewood Cliffs, N.J.: Prentice-Hall.

Coles, R. 1993. *The call of service.* New York: Houghton Mifflin Company.

Collins, G. R. 1993. *Excellence and ethics in counseling.* Carol Stream, Ill.: Word Publishing.

Colston, L. G. 1969. *Judgment in pastoral counseling.* Nashville: Abingdon Press.

Couture, P. D., and R. J. Hunter, eds. 1995. *Pastoral care and social conflict.* Nashville: Abingdon Press.

Culbertson, P. L. 1994. *Counseling men.* Minneapolis: Fortress Press.

Culbertson, P. L., and A. B. Shippee, eds. 1990. *The pastor: Readings from the patristic period.* Minneapolis: Fortress Press.

de Shazer, S. 1985. *Keys to solution in brief therapy.* New York: Norton.

Ehrenreich, B. 1990. *Fear of falling.* New York: HarperPerennial.

———.1996. In defense of splitting up. *Time* 147(15) (April 8): 80.

Ellison, M. M. 1994. Common decency: A new Christian sexual Ethics. In *Sexuality and the sacred: Sources for theological reflection,* ed. J. Nelson and S. Longfellow. Louisville, Ky.: Westminster/John Knox Press.

Ellul, J. 1974. Work and calling. In *Callings,* ed. J. Holloway and W. Campbell, 18–44. New York: Paulist Press.

Epictetus. 1909. The golden sayings of Epictetus. In The Harvard Classics, vol. 2, ed. C. Elliot, 115–84. New York: Collier and Son.

Fassel, D. 1990. *Working ourselves to death: The high cost of workaholism, the rewards of recovery.* San Francisco: Harper.

Fortune, M. M. 1983. *Sexual violence.* New York: The Pilgrim Press.

———. 1989. *Is nothing sacred? When sex invades the pastoral relationship.* HarperSanFrancisco.

———. 1992. *Clergy misconduct: Sexual abuse in the ministerial relationship.* Seattle, Wash.: The Center for the Prevention of Sexual and Domestic Violence.

Fox, M. 1983. *Original blessing.* Santa Fe, N. Mex.: Bear and Company.

———. 1994. *The reinvention of work.* New York: HarperCollins Publishers.

Furstenburg F., and A. Cherlin. 1991. *Divided families: What happens to children when parents part.* Cambridge, Mass.: Harvard University Press.

Gallagher, M. 1996. *The abolition of marriage.* Washington, D.C.: Regnery Publishing, Inc.

Galston, W. A. 1996. Divorce American style. *The Public Interest* 124 (Summer): 12–15.

Gerkin, C. V. 1986. *Widening the horizons: Pastoral responses to a fragmented society.* Philadelphia: Westminster Press.

Gibbs, N. 1989. How America has run out of time. *Time* (April 24): 58–61.

Gilligan, C. 1982. *In a different voice: Psychological theory and women's development.* Cambridge, Mass.: Harvard University Press.

Godbey, G., and J. Robinson. 1995. Are average Americans really overworked? *The American Enterprise* 6(5) (September-October): 43.

Grant, B. W. 1982. *From sin to wholeness.* Philadelphia: Westminster Press.

Greeley, A. 1994. Marital infidelity. *Society* 31(4) (May-June): 9–13.

Gregory the Great. 1995. *The book of pastoral rule.* Trans. James Barmby. Vol. 12 of A Select Library of the Nicene and Post-Nicene Fathers of the Christian Church, 2d ser., ed. Henry Wace and Philip Schaff, 1–72. Peabody, Mass.: Hendrickson Publishers.

Grenz, S. J., and R. D. Bell. 1995. *Betrayal of trust: Sexual misconduct in the pastorate.* Downer's Grove, Ill.: Intervarsity Press.

Gula, R. 1996. *Ethics in pastoral ministry.* New York: Paulist Press.

Gutiérrez, G. 1973. *A theology of liberation.* New York: Orbis.

Harmon, N. B. 1978. *Ministerial ethics and etiquette.* Nashville: Abingdon Press.

Hauerwas, S. 1983. *Peaceable kingdom.* Notre Dame, Ind.: University of Notre Dame Press.

———. 1988. *Christian existence today.* Durham, N.C.: Labyrinth Press.

Height, A. D. 1997. Padded prowess: A Veblenian interpretation of the long hours of salaried workers. *Journal of Economic Issues* 31(1) (March): 29–38.

Hendrix, H. 1988. *Getting the love you want.* New York: Henry Holt and Company.

Heschel, A. J. 1951. *The Sabbath.* New York: Farrar, Strauss, & Young.

Heyward, C. 1987. *Touching our strength: The erotic as power and the love of God.* San Francisco: Harper & Row.

Heyward, C., and M. Fortune. 1994. Boundaries or barriers? An exchange. *The Christian Century* 111(18) (June 1): 579–82.

Hiltner, S. 1949. *Pastoral counseling.* Nashville: Abingdon Press.

———. 1953. *Sex ethics and the Kinsey Report.* New York: Association Press.

Hochschild, A. R. 1989. *The second shift.* New York: Avon.

———. 1997a. There's no place like work. *The New York Times Magazine.* Section 6 (April 20): 51–55, 81, 84.

————.1997b. *The time bind: When work becomes home and home becomes work.* New York: Henry Holt and Company.

Hoffman, J. C. 1979. *Ethical confrontation in counseling.* Chicago: The University of Chicago Press.

Kennedy, T. D. 1994. Can war be just? In *From Christ to the world,* ed. W. G. Boulton, T. D. Kennedy, and A. Verhey, 436–42. Grand Rapids, Mich.: Eerdmans.

Kohak, E. 1984. *The embers and the stars: A philosophical inquiry into the moral sense of nature.* Chicago: University of Chicago Press.

Killinger, B. 1991. *Workaholics: The respectable addicts.* New York: Simon & Schuster.

Lebacqz, K. 1985. *Professional ethics: Power and paradox.* Nashville: Abingdon Press.

Lebacqz, K., and R. G. Barton. 1991. *Sex in the parish.* Louisville, Ky.: Westminster/John Knox Press.

Linder, S. 1970. *The harried leisure class.* New York: Columbia University Press.

Lovin, R. W. 1995. *Reinhold Niebuhr and Christian Realism.* Cambridge: Cambridge University Press.

McFague, S. 1993. *The body of God: An ecological theology.* Minneapolis: Fortress Press.

Michael, R. T., J. H. Gagnon, E. O. Laumann, and G. Kolata. 1994. *Sex in America.* Canada: Little, Brown & Company.

Miles, R. L. 1995. *Ethics and transcendence: Reinhold Niebuhr, Rosemary Ruether, and Sharon Welch.* Ph.D. diss., The University of Chicago.

Minirth, F., D. Hawkins, P. Meier, and R. Flournoy. 1986. *How to beat burnout.* Chicago: Moody Press.

Nazianzen, G. 1995. Oration two: A defense of his flight to Pontus. In *Select orations,* trans. Charles G. Browne. Vol. 7, A Select Library of the Nicene and Post-Nicene Fathers of the Christian Church, 2d ser., ed. Henry Wace and Philip Schaff, 204–27. Peabody, Mass.: Hendrickson Publishers.

Nelson, J. B. 1979. *Embodiment: An approach to sexuality and Christian theology.* Minneapolis: Augsburg Publishing House.

————. 1992. *Body theology.* Louisville Ky.: Westminster/John Knox Press.

Niebuhr, H. R. 1943. *Radical monotheism.* New York: Harper & Row.

————. 1963. *The responsible self.* New York: Harper & Row.

Niebuhr, R. 1937. *Beyond tragedy: Essays on the Christian interpretation of history.* New York: Charles Scribner's Sons.

————. 1941. *The nature and destiny of man: A Christian interpretation.* Vol. 1. New York: Charles Scribner's Sons.

Noyce, G. 1987. *The minister as moral counselor.* Nashville: Abingdon Press.

————. 1988. *Pastoral ethics: Professional responsibilities of the clergy.* Nashville: Abingdon.

Nussbaum, M. 1986. *The fragility of goodness: Luck and ethics in Greek tragedy and philosophy.* Cambridge: Cambridge University Press.

Oates, W. 1966. *Pastoral counseling in social problems: Extremism, race, sex, divorce.* Philadelphia: Westminster Press.

————. 1971. *Confessions of a workaholic: The facts about work addiction.* New York: World.

Oden, T. C. 1984. *Care of souls in the classic tradition.* Philadelphia: Fortress Press.

——. 1986. *Crisis ministries.* Classical Pastoral Care Series, vol. 4. Grand Rapids, Mich.: Baker Books.

——. 1987. *Becoming a minister.* Classical Pastoral Care Series, vol. 1. Grand Rapids, Mich.: Baker Books.

——. 1989a. *Ministry through word and sacrament.* Classical Pastoral Care Series, vol. 2. Grand Rapids, Mich.: Baker Books.

——. 1989b. *Pastoral counsel.* Classical Pastoral Care Series, vol. 3. Grand Rapids, Mich.: Baker Books.

O'Hanlon, W., and M. Weiner-Davis. 1989. *In search of solutions: A new direction in psychotherapy.* New York: Norton.

Patton, J., and B. Childs. 1988. *Christian marriage and family: Caring for our generations.* Nashville: Abingdon.

Pellauer, M. D., B. Chester, and J. Boyajian, eds. 1987. *Sexual assault and abuse: A handbook for clergy and religious professionals.* San Francisco: Harper & Row.

Peyser, M. 1997. Time bind? What time bind? *Newsweek* 129(19) (May 12): 69.

Poling, J. 1991. Ethics in pastoral care and counseling. In *Handbook for basic types of pastoral care and counseling,* ed. H. W. Stone and W. Clements. Nashville: Abingdon Press.

Powers, M. 1997. The hidden costs of divorce. *Human Ecology Forum* 25(1) (Winter): 4–7.

Raines, J. C., and D. C. Day-Lower. 1986. *Modern work and human meaning.* Philadelphia: Westminster Press.

Rifkin, J. 1995. Work. *UTNE Reader* (69) (May-June): 53–62.

Robinson, K. 1994. Which side are you on? *The Family Therapy Networker* 18(3) (May/June): 19–30.

Ruether, R. R. 1983. *Sexism and God talk: Toward a feminist theology.* Boston: Beacon Press.

——. 1992. *Gaia and God: An ecofeminist theology of Earth-healing.* HarperSanFrancisco.

Ruether, R. R., and E. Bianchi. 1976. *From machismo to mutuality: Essays on sexism and woman-man liberation.* New York: Paulist Press.

Ryken, L. 1995. *Redeeming the time.* Grand Rapids, Mich.: Baker Book House Company.

Schlessinger, L. 1995. *Ten stupid things women do to mess up their lives.* New York: HarperPerennial.

——. 1996. *How could you do that?!* New York: HarperCollins Publishers.

Schor, J. B. 1993. *The overworked American: The unexpected decline of leisure.* New York: BasicBooks.

Shapiro, L. 1997. The myth of quality time. *Newsweek* 129(19) (May 12): 62–69.

Shelp, E. E. 1994. AIDS, high-risk behaviors, and moral judgments. In *Sexuality and the sacred: Sources for theological reflection,* ed. J. Nelson and S. Longfellow. Louisville, Ky.: Westminster/John Knox Press.

Stone, H. W. 1993. *Crisis counseling.* Minneapolis: Fortress Press.

——. 1994. *Brief pastoral counseling: Short-term approaches and strategies.* Minneapolis: Fortress Press.

————. 1996. *Theological context for pastoral caregiving*. New York: The Haworth Press.

Stroup, H. W., and N. S. Wood. 1974. *Sexuality and the counseling pastor*. Philadelphia: Fortress Press.

Sykes, J. B., ed. 1976. *The concise Oxford dictionary*. Oxford: The Clarendon Press.

Talbot, M. 1997. Love, American style: What the alarmists about divorce don't get about idealism in America. *The New Republic* 216(15) (April 14): 30–38.

Terkel, S. 1972. *Working: People talk about what they do all day and how they feel about what they do*. New York: The New Press.

Trull, J. E., and J. E. Carter. 1993. *Ministerial ethics: Being a good minister in a not-so-good world*. Nashville: Broadman and Holman Publishers.

Ventura, M. 1995. The age of interruption. *The Family Therapy Networker* 19(1) (January/February): 19–25, 28–31.

Volf, M. 1991. *Work in the Spirit*. New York: Oxford University Press, Inc.

Waldman, S. 1996. The case against divorce. *Washington Monthly* 28(1) (January/February): 37–38.

Wallerstein, J. S. 1995. *The good marriage: How and why love lasts*. Boston: Houghton Mifflin.

Wallerstein, J. S., and S. Blakeslee. 1989. *Second chances: Men, women, and children a decade after divorce*. New York: Ticknor & Fields.

Walljasper, J. 1997. The speed trap. *UTNE Reader* (March-April): 41–47.

Ware, K. 1995. Marriage and divorce: An orthodox perspective. In *A Textbook of Christian Ethics*, ed. Robin Gill, 522–33. Edinburgh: T & T Clark.

Weeks, L. B. 1987. *Making ethical decisions: A casebook*. Philadelphia: Westminster Press.

Weiner-Davis, M. 1992. *Divorce busting*. New York: Simon & Schuster.

Whitehead, B. D. 1997. *The divorce culture*. New York: Alfred A. Knopf.

Wiest, W. E., and E. A. Smith. 1990. *Ethics in ministry: A guide for the professional*. Minneapolis: Fortress Press.

Wind, J., R. Burck, P. Camenisch, and D. McCann, eds. 1991. *Clergy ethics in a changing society: Mapping the terrain*. Louisville, Ky.: Westminster/John Knox Press.

Zinsmeister, K. 1997. Divorces' toll on children. *Current* (February): 29–33.